Heinz-Sigurd Raethel

The New Duck Handbook

Ornamental and Domestic Ducks
Everything About Housing, Care, Feeding
Diseases, and Breeding

With a Special Chapter on Commercial Uses of Ducks

With 30 Color Photographs by Eminent Animal Photographers and 30 Drawings by Fritz W. Kohler

Consulting Editor:
Matthew M. Vriends, PhD

Translated from the German by Rita and Robert Kimber

The title of the German book is *Enten*

All inquiries should be addressed to:
Barron's Educational Series, Inc.
250 Wireless Boulevard
Hauppauge, NY 11788

Library of Congress Catalog Card No. 88-36698

International Standard Book No. 0-8120-4088-0

Library of Congress Cataloging-in-Publication Data

Raethel, Heinz-Sigurd.
The new duck handbook: ornamental and domestic ducks: everything about housing, care, feeding, diseases, and breeding, with a special chapter on commercial uses of ducks / Heinz-Sigurd Raethel; translated by Rita and Rober Kimber: American consulting editor, Matthew M. Vriends.
Translation of: Enten. Includes index.
ISBN 0-8120-4088-0
1. Ducks. I. title.
SF505.R1713 1988
636.5'97—dc19 88-36698
CIP

Printed and Bound in Hong Kong

2 4900 98765432

Front cover: Red-crested Pochard (drake)
Inside front cover: Mallard drake rising from the water
Inside back cover: American Pekin Ducks
Back cover: (above, left) A girl with baby ducklings; (above, middle) Wood Duck (drake); (above, right) European Pochard (drake). (center, left) Mallard mother duck with babies; (center, right) Mallard drake. (below, left) European Wigeon; (below, right) Domestic duck.

Photo credits:
Danegger: pp. 53, lower, and 79, upper right; inside front cover; back cover, upper middle); Maier: p. 80; Meyers: back cover, center left; Pott: p. 18, upper left and right; p. 35, lower; p. 53, upper right); p. 79, center, left; front cover; back cover, center right; Reinhard: p. 53, upper left; inside back cover; back cover, upper left and lower right and left; Scherz: p. 35, upper; Skogstad: back cover, upper right); Wolters: pp. 17, 36, 54; Wothe: p. 18, lower; p. 79, upper left and center left and lower left and right.

About the Author:
Dr. Heinz-Sigurd Raethel is a retired director of veterinary services and has for many years been on the board of trustees of the Zoological Garden of Berlin in the capacity of scientific advisor. His major interest has always been ducks—their behavior, how to keep them in captivity, and how to breed them—with a special focus on ornamental ducks. He is the author of several books on birds and many publications in scientific journals.

Important note:
This book gives advice on buying, keeping, and breeding ducks. Ducks whose flight is not restricted can wreak havoc in a carefully landscaped pond in a neighbor's garden. Ducks should therefore be rendered flightless (see page 37).
As protection for your own family as well as for others, you should build an adequate fence around your duck pond, especially if there are small children in your household.
Liability insurance that covers the duck pond is highly recommended.
Any keeper of ducks has to make sure that no water from the pond will drain onto neighboring property, whether above ground or below. It is therefore important to check the drainage pipe regularly and to change the water or empty the pond correctly (see page 38).
Domestic ducks are not allowed on the waters of fish hatcheries and spawning grounds or in nature preserves.
Duck keepers who plan to sell duck meat and especially duck eggs should familiarize themselves with pertinent health regulations (see pages 59 and 60).

Contents

Contents

Preface

Ducks are found all over the world, and everyone knows what they look like. You may see them on a pond in a park or on rivers and lakes, or you can go to a zoo to admire the many different, beautiful kinds there are. Keepers of ducks distinguish between "ornamental" and "utility" or "commercial" ducks. Ornamental ducks are for animal lovers who like having these birds around for their beauty, while utility ducks are kept for the meat, eggs, and down they produce. In this book the many questions often asked by beginning duck keepers—as well as by those who have had ducks for some time—are answered knowledgeably and in detail. Its author, Dr. Heinz-Sigurd Raethel, worked for many years as a veterinarian at the Veterinary Laboratory in Berlin, Germany, and was scientific advisor for the board of trustees of the Berlin Zoological Garden. The breeding and behavior of ducks has always been of interest to him, and in this book he is sharing his knowledge and experience.

The author's advice on buying ducks will help you choose the right kind of bird, whether you are interested in breeding, commercial use, or simple enjoyment. Since ducks are often shipped, the author discusses the transporting of birds in some detail. Ducks can't do without water, and the chapter "Housing and Environment" therefore discusses different ways of supplying this basic element, ranging from natural bodies of water to small artificial ponds. Detailed instructions and informative drawings show how to build and equip an artificial duck pond, a duck shelter, a duck house, as well as an aviary.

Since ducks are omnivorous and far from fussy eaters, picking out a good diet for them from among many possible foods is not difficult. Describing the different feeding methods appropriate for ornamental ducks, breeding ducks, and market ducks takes up more space. The chapter "Health Care and Diseases" gives detailed descriptions of sicknesses that can occur even among ducks that are fed and cared for properly. The information on breeding ducks is equally extensive and informative, including discussions of the difference between natural and artificial incubation and of the hatching and development of baby ducklings. A special chapter discusses the commercial uses of ducks and explains what to do with their meat and eggs.

The chapter on the behavior of ducks is especially interesting. The author describes the rituals of bathing and preening; the molting period, when the ducks are especially vulnerable; the behavior during courtship and between established mates; nest building; and incubation. Accompanying the text are numerous drawings that illustrate the "language of ducks." Finally, the most popular species of ornamental ducks and the most common utility ducks are introduced in a lengthy chapter. The descriptions of the breeds and species include information on origin, appearance, habitat, requirements in captivity, breeding, number of eggs laid, rate of growth, and weight. Many of the ducks described are also shown in excellent color photos.

The author and the publisher wish to thank all those who have contributed to this book, especially the photographers for their beautiful color photos and Fritz W. Köhler for his beautiful and informative drawings.

Considerations Before You Buy

We don't kow how much Walt Disney knew about the nature of real ducks when he created his immortal Donald Duck along with his entourage of no-less-famous relatives. In any case, this comical bird with its broad bill and even broader behind (the whole tribe is bare-bottomed) has become a symbol of the philistine and the eternal loser without being the least bit unsympathetic.

Ducks appear in fairy tales only rarely and then as figures of metamorphosis, always in connection, of course, with water. In one of the tales by the Grimm brothers, called "Fundevogel" or "Bird-foundling," a girl versed in magic transforms her friend into a pond and herself into a duck swimming on the pond. When the evil cook, who sees through the trick, tries to drink the pond dry, the duck grabs her by the head and drags her into the water, where the old witch drowns.

People were interested in ducks as early as 2,000 B.C., as old pictorial representations show. Ducks were raised and fattened in ancient China, Egypt, and Rome, but the earliest reports of systematic domestication date back only to the period of the Carolingians.

Ducks have been depicted in the visual arts throughout the ages in various forms: They appear in the spare style of the Egyptians, as an ornamental element in Greek art, as symbols of a feeling for nature in Japanese art, and as striking, colorful accents in Dutch genre painting in the seventeenth century. And in our day the carved wooden decoys that were originally used in duck hunting have become sought-after collector's items.

Ornamental or Utility Ducks?

When you decide to keep ducks you should be clear about what kind of ducks you really want. Duck keepers speak of ornamental and utility or commercial ducks. What is meant by these terms?

Ornamental ducks, in the language of duck fanciers, means any wild duck species. These ducks are kept as "ornaments" because of their beautiful plumage and their interesting behavior. They are not expected to bring an economic return but are kept strictly for the pleasure of watching them.

Ornamental and utility ducks are kept for different reasons. Ornamental breeds, such as the mallard (above), are kept purely for esthetic reasons; utility ducks, such as the crested duck (below), yield meat, eggs, and feathers.

Utility or commercial ducks are various breeds of domestic ducks. Their owners expect to get an economic return in the form of meat, eggs, and down feathers.

Here are a couple more specialized terms:

- *Market ducks* are commercial ducks that are being fattened for market;
- *Breeding ducks* are kept strictly for the production of more ducks.

Ducks for Beginners

As everyone knows, practice makes perfect. This saying should be kept in mind by the beginning duck keeper as well. A duck enthusiast should start his or her new hobby on a modest scale and not take big risks at the beginning. That is why this book does not discuss any species or breed that makes difficult demands. There is hardly a more discouraging experience than embarking on a new venture only to encounter failure. In the chapter "Ornamental Ducks and Utility Ducks" (see page 72) you will find which breeds and species are especially suitable for beginners and what special qualities distinguish them.

What Ducks Need to Thrive

There are a few basic questions you should consider before you go out to buy ducks.

Basic Needs

Knowing the basic needs of an animal is a prerequisite for the proper care of that animal. Just about everybody knows that ducks are waterfowl and that their essential element is water. Accordingly, all ducks in captivity should have water to swim in to be happy. This is correct in principle. All ornamental and most utility ducks need to be able to swim if they are to survive. But there is no rule without an exception. People have bred some strains, such as the Indian runner, the Orpington, the Campbell, and the American Pekin duck, which can manage without a pond as long as they have an opportunity for bathing.

Space Requirement

Ornamental ducks need more space than domestic ducks, so don't make the mistake many beginners make of getting carried away by the beauty of the ducks and buying out of sheer enthusiasm. Always consider first how much space you have available for your future charges. Neither ornamental nor commercial ducks like being crowded together in their runs and shelters with others of their own or related species (see Housing and Environment, page 13).

Noise

There is one thing the beginning duck fancier hardly ever thinks about ahead of time, and that is the noise the birds will make, which may well disturb and annoy neighbors. There are not too many people who respond by saying, "I like to hear ducks quacking because it reminds me of my childhood in the country." But not all ducks quack constantly and loudly all year round. Among the ornamental species, only the mallard and the spotbill duck tend to be very noisy; most of the others use their relatively soft voices only during the few weeks of courtship.

Commercial ducks on the whole quack rather loudly. But here, too, there is an exception, the muscovy duck. This utility duck, which was bred from a South American wild species, is almost silent and is guaranteed not to annoy any neighbors.

Time Investment

Looking after ducks does not require a massive time commitment. Chores include daily feeding; cleaning the ground in the run, and, in the winter, the floor of the shelter or house; and changing the water in the swimming basin, which in most cases doesn't have to be done every day. The water has to be changed more frequently only if the basin is very small and the run is crowded. Natural streams and ponds that maintain a biological equilibrium don't require any cleaning at all except for the removal of an occasional dead fish or mouse and other decaying organic matter that may turn up. You should figure on spending an average of one and a half to two hours a day on your ducks. But keep in mind that this book is intended for amateur and hobby breeders, not for commercial enterprises where birds are kept on a large scale and where, obviously, different rules apply (see Daily Chores, page 38).

Feeding

Neither commercial nor ornamental ducks are difficult to feed. Ducks are omnivores and like lots of things. In fact, they are sometimes referred to as the "pigs of the bird world." If you don't have much time, you can buy commercial rations of various composition for baby ducklings, breeding ducks, or market ducks and use them for ornamental as well as utility ducks. If you have more time, you can compose your own duck rations (see Diet, page 22).

Supervision

If for no other reason than self-interest, you will want to keep a watchful eye over your ducks to prevent anything bad from happening to them. This supervision includes making sure that all the birds get their share of food, that the smaller and weaker ones are not shoved aside, let alone persecuted by the bigger ones, and that sick birds do not go unnoticed (see Health Care and Diseases, page 40).

Vacation Care

Remember that there may be times when you want to take a vacation away from home. When that happens you will need to find some kindly person who will take good care of your ducks. But it's not always easy to find such a person, especially at the last minute. So look for a good caretaker for your birds ahead of time, and have him or her do the chores with you for a day or two before you take off for vacation.

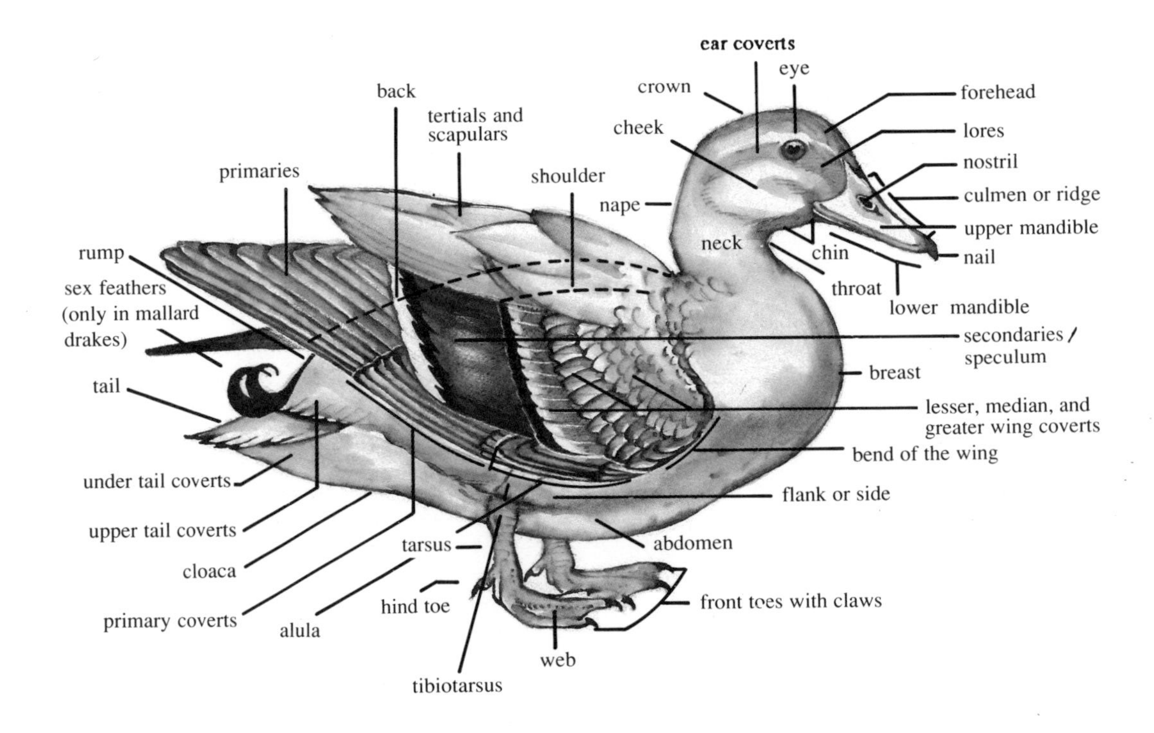

It is important for a keeper of ducks to know the birds' different body parts.

Advice For Buying Ducks

The Right Duck for Every Situation

Someone interested in keeping ducks is in the fortunate position of having a great variety to choose from. Whether you are looking for ornamental ducks that will give you esthetic pleasure or whether you are motivated by the more utilitarian desire for meat or eggs, you will almost always find a duck that answers your desires.

Preening. A duck preens itself carefully, especially after bathing, to maintain the insulating property of its plumage. For the feathers to stay water repellent they have to be properly arranged and oiled frequently with the secretion of the oil gland.

For Esthetic Pleasure

A good way to familiarize yourself with the many different species of ducks and compare them is to visit zoological gardens, where there are almost always bodies of water populated with many of these waterfowl.

Small species like the mandarin duck, wood duck, green-winged teal, garganey, Bahama pintail, and Baikal teal are especially well suited for living in small aviaries and on garden ponds.

Large species like the pintail, gadwall, falcated teal, red-crested pochard, and the wigeon should not be crowded together in a small area.

Diving ducks should be avoided unless the body of water you have for them is at least 32 to 40 inches (80–100 cm) deep.

For Breeding

If you hope to breed ornamental ducks, you should not keep the birds in small, crowded quarters. The fewer pairs share the limited space of an aviary or a garden pond, the sooner they are likely to breed (see Keeping Ducks in an Aviary and Keeping Ducks on a Pond, page 33).

If you are keeping purebred utility ducks, you should restrict yourself to one breed per coop or run (see Raising Ducks, page 46). It is impossible to obtain purebred offspring if several breeds are kept together. A place to swim is essential for breeding most commercial breeds, for they can successfully mate only in the water (see Matrimony, page 69).

For Commercial Use

Meat is the primary commercial product of ducks, but there is also a use for duck feathers and duck eggs (see Commercial Uses of Ducks, page 59). Utility ducks are usually exhibited at poultry shows.

How Many Ducks?

Wild or ornamental ducks are monogamous. They are therefore always kept in pairs, although you can house several pairs of the same or related species together.

Domestic or utility ducks have lost their monogamous way of life in the long course of domestication, and if breeding is the goal, a drake is kept together with several females. But there should be no more than five females per drake so that as many of the eggs as possible are fertilized. You should never attempt to house several drakes and their harems together in the same enclosure. The drakes would promptly start fighting over the females, which is bound to have a negative effect on the breeding operation.

Advice For Buying Ducks

Ducklings: The main economic use of ducks is to fatten and sell the ducklings of both sexes. Since these birds are ready for slaughter before they reach sexual maturity, they can all be kept together in the same space as long as it is adequate for their numbers. Allow enough room, for ducklings that are raised for market grow fast and will soon need quite a bit more space than they did when first purchased (see A Large Duck House, page 19).

Where To Buy Ducks

Breeders: The great majority of duck owners are inspired to embark on their hobby after a visit to the duck section of a poultry show. At these exhibitions mostly commercial breeds are shown; ornamental ducks are less often entered. When you see a type of duck you like, you can usually buy some from the breeder who is exhibiting the birds.

Poultry Magazines: The advertisement sections of poultry magazines always carry a lot of ads for ornamental as well as commercial ducks. Ducks are usually sold as baby ducklings or as young birds. It is safest, of course, to pick up the birds at the seller's because this way you get a chance to look them over and make sure that they are healthy and active. But in many cases you will have to have them shipped to you (see The Transport, page 11).

How To Tell If a Duck Is Healthy

You can assess a duck's state of health by looking for certain signs.

Behavior: A healthy duck looks at the world with bright, lively eyes and tries to get away from people. This is especially true when it has just arrived at its new home.

Plumage: The plumage should be smooth and clean, especially in the vent area. A new duck may be dirty because it soiled itself out of fear during the trip, which should, of course, not be interpreted as a sign of illness.

Feet: The feet also should be smooth, and there should be no calluses, let alone sores, on the underside of the toes.

State of Nutrition: You can judge the state of nutrition by feeling the bird's breast region. The breast muscles should be well developed.

Ducks that are sick or not properly nourished have a narrow breastbone that protrudes sharply. However, this test does not work with baby ducklings and recently fledged ducklings. Their breast muscles are not yet fully developed at this age; consequently the breastbone will not be well covered regardless of the state of the birds nutrition and health.

The Age of Ducks

Ornamental or wild ducks can live 12 to 15 years. Most fanciers acquire them as young adult birds when their sex is already obvious from the color of the plumage (see The Molt, a Time of Vulnerability, page 67). But sometimes older ducks that are reliable breeders come up for sale and are worth buying because wild ducks can breed until they are quite old. Still, you should make it a practice never to not buy any kind of ducks that are more than 6 years old.

Domestic or commercial ducks are always slaughtered before they reach their potential maximum age,.

Generally, commercial ducks are purchased by producers as day-old chicks. If you plan to breed ducks, it is best to buy the birds in the late summer or in the fall because they are strongest then and usually cheapest, too. They should not be older than two years.

When it comes to the age of fully grown ducks, all you have to go on is the seller's word because there is no way of checking an adult duck's age.It is always best to deal with reputable breeders.

Advice For Buying Ducks

The Transport

Shipping Containers

Ducks are shipped in crates, baskets, and cardboard boxes. Because they defecate out of fear during transport, disposable boxes of heavy cardboard are used for short trips. Duck chicks are usually shipped in similar cardboard boxes. If the trip lasts for more than a day, it is best to use wooden crates whose tops are padded with burlap or cotton to prevent the birds from scraping their heads. The crates should not be too roomy so that if the birds panic and start dashing around frantically they cannot injure themselves or trample each other to death. If several birds are to be shipped together, it is safer in any case to subdivide a large crate so that each duck has its own compartment. Baby ducklings are usually shipped in round cardboard boxes that hold five chicks apiece.

Food and Water

For short trips no food is necessary. First of all, ducks don't starve that quickly, and secondly, they are much too nervous to eat during transport. For longer shipping that may take more than three days, food troughs are mounted on the inside walls of the crates and filled with grain that has been soaked in water or with finely chopped greens.

Caution: Ducks are unable to eat dry food because they have to moisten it first with water. Soft foods that contain bread or potatoes sour too quickly.

The crates also have to be equipped with water dishes. But don't simply fill the dishes with water—it would spill very quickly. Instead, carefully fasten to the dish a large coarse sponge soaked full of water.

Preparing the Shipping Container

A shipping container for live animals has to have enough large, round air holes to keep the animals inside from suffocating. The bottom should consist of an absorbent material, such as several thicknesses of filter paper with a layer of straw on top. A large label with the words "Caution! Live Poultry!" in easily legible lettering should be securely affixed to the outside of the container to alert shipping personnel to the contents.

Method of Shipping

For short distances, the birds should be shipped at night if at all possible. If you use the mail or railroad shipping, always send live animals by express. Inform the receiving party in good time when the ducks are due to arrive. It happens more often than one likes to think that live animals sit around in their boxes unclaimed for days in the baggage rooms of airports or the package departments of railroad stations and post offices because the addressee was not notified in time.

Arrival at the Destination

Before you accept a shipment you should always check in the presence of the postal clerk or shipping company official that the animals are alive and well and that they are the species or breed you ordered.

The law specifies that even if there is no explicit statement to that effect, the seller is responsible for any significant visible or hidden defects in goods found at the time of transfer. If the buyer can prove that the purchased animals were already sick or infected with disease carriers when they were shipped or at the moment of transfer of ownership, he or she has the right during a six-month period to annul the purchase or to request a new shipment of animals at a reduced price—or, in some situations, to ask for damages.

If a disease is noticed, the buyer has to have proof that the animal in question is the one he bought. Foot rings can be such proof of identity, or a statement by the postal official at the time of delivery. Otherwise proof of identity is difficult. If the buyer wants to collect damages, a veterinarian or a veterinary laboratory has to ascertain what the disease was and the cause of death.

Unpacking

After you unpack the ducks, clean off the soiled and sticky parts of the plumage with a soft sponge and lukewarm water. The ducks themselves will later do a thorough cleaning of their plumage. If the new arrivals are the sole occupants of the shelter and the run, and if the weather is clement, you can release the ducks immediately into their new home, assuming that they look healthy. Watch them swim for a while to make sure that their plumage is properly water repellant so that they won't drown (see Dry Plumage, page 42).

Housing and Environment

An Artificial Duck Pond

It makes sense to build your duck pond somewhere where you can conveniently watch your ducks. This is usually near a terrace or a window. A spot underneath trees is not recommended. First of all, removing the dead leaves in the fall is a major chore; a more serious consideration is that the pressure of tree roots (especially of fast-growing species) may cause leaks in the walls of the pond. I would therefore urge you to pick a sunny but protected location.

The walls of the pond can be made of concrete or of heavy plastic. The following sections give some general advice on constructing ponds, and you can find more detailed instructions in some of the books listed in the bibliography on page 93.

Ponds Made of Concrete

Preparation: Mark the outlines of the pond with wooden stakes in the exact spot where the pond is to be located. Two pairs of ornamental ducks should have a pond measuring about 30 to 40 square feet (3–4 square meters). The depth of the excavation is made up of the water depth required by the ducks plus the thickness of the concrete bottom. You will have to dig down

- at least 24 inches plus 14 inches (60 plus 35 cm) for dabbling ducks, and
- 40 plus 14 inches (1 m plus 35 cm) for diving ducks.

One side of the pond should have a very gentle slope so that the ducks can climb in and out of the water easily. The bottom of the excavation should be pounded smooth and hard all over. Large rocks and thick roots have to be removed because they might later cause cracks in the concrete. If the soil is too loose, cover it with gravel or broken bricks, which are then stamped into the ground.

Pouring the Concrete: You make concrete by

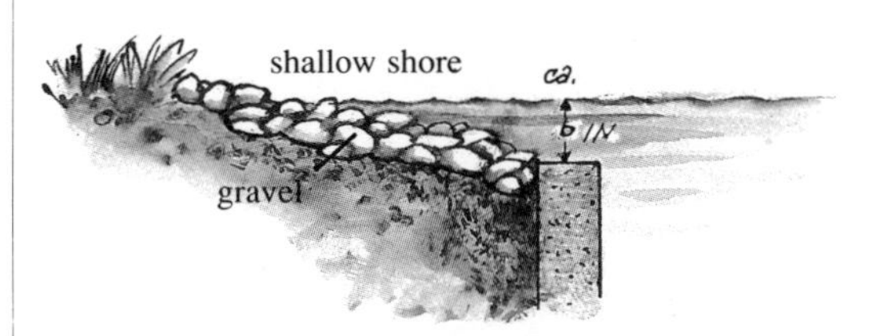

Building a duck pond. The edge of the pond has to be made very shallow on one side and covered with gravel.

mixing 1 part dry Portland cement with 5 parts sand. Then add enough water mixed with a sealer to get consistency of stiff dough.The usual proportion of sealer to water is 1 to 30. Build layers of concrete up to 6 inches (15 cm), working in strips or "forms" rather than covering the entire area all at once. Smooth the surface with a board. Since wet concrete tends not to keep its shape on sloping walls, you should place a layer of wire mesh over it to give it a solid "corset." In some places strips of wire mesh will overlap, and these seams should be weighted down with bricks. Then add a second 6-inch layer of cement, smooth it, and remove the bricks as you go along. To prevent the concrete from drying too quickly, cover each form immediately with damp sand, and spread damp cloths over the edges of the pond. Keep both the sand and the cloths damp, and don't remove them until the concrete has set. Finally, fill in the pores of the rough concrete walls with mortar (1 part cement to 3 parts sand with enough water to make a spreadable mixture) and smooth the surface with a board.

The Drain: Ducks dirty the water, and it must therefore be replenished continually. A good drain is essential for this. When the concrete walls of the pond are poured, a 3-inch drainpipe with a brass-screw fitting has to be set in the deepest spot. The drainpipe has to be laid at a downward angle and connected to the sewage system. You should seek the advice of a plumber for this job. When the pond is ready to be filled, an overflow pipe is screwed into the fitting at the bottom. The top of the overflow

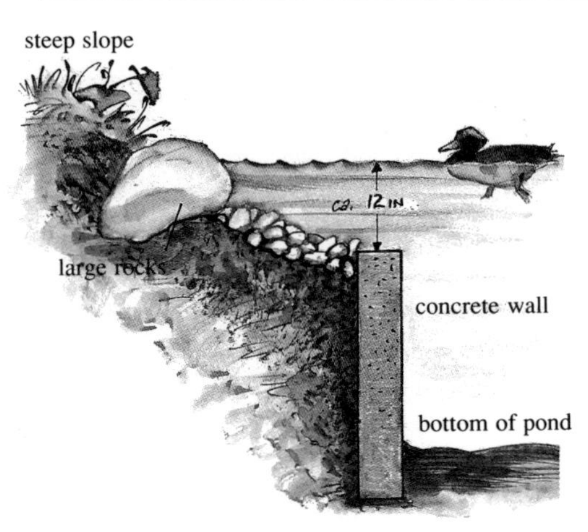

A steep shore has to be secured against mud slides with large rocks. Set the rocks into the earth at a slight upward angle.

pipe has a perforated cap or is covered with screening. In this way, flooding is avoided when the water surface rises, as it does after heavy rains, and the drain cannot get plugged up with feathers, leaves, or large particles of dirt (see drawing opposite). To prevent frost damage, the water is drained out of the pond for the winter.

Ponds Made of Plastic

The great advantage of plastic over concrete is that it can expand more than ice and will consequently not suffer frost damage. A plastic pond does not need to be drained during winter.

Preparation: Excavate the site of the pond just as you would for a concrete pond. Clean the surface carefully and smooth it because pointed objects can damage the plastic. Make sure the place where the ducks get in and out of the pond has a very slight slope because the plastic can get extremely slippery when algae develop on it. Be sure you use plastic designed exclusively for building ponds. (This kind of liner—usually made of butyl rubber or PVC—is available at stores specializing in materials for pond construction, at garden centers, and at some pet-supply stores.) The plastic comes in rolls of different widths and should be at least 0.03 inch (0.75 mm) thick. Calculate ahead of time how much plastic you need and take into account that the plastic has to reach about 1 foot (30 cm) beyond the edges of the pool.

Putting Down the Plastic: If a single sheet of plastic is not large enough for the entire pond, strips of plastic have to be glued together with a chemical

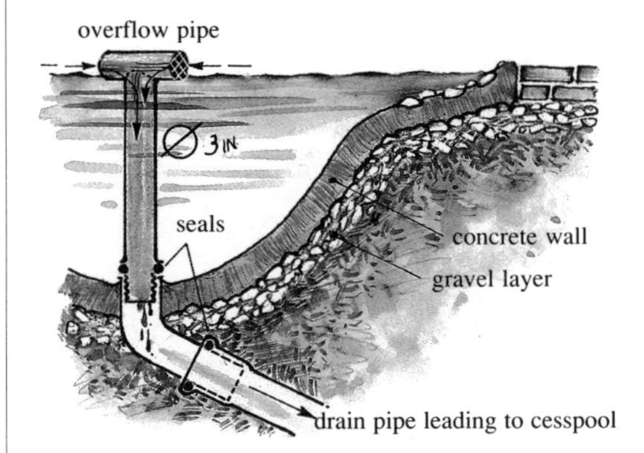

Drainage. A drainage pipe with an overflow pipe is recommended. The drainage pipe should be connected to a sewage system.

that welds the edges together. Ask the salesperson where you are buying the plastic for advice. Spread out the plastic sheet next to the excavation for the pond and carefully pull it over the hole, making sure that the protruding rim is about the same width all around (about 12 inches [30 cm]). Then start running water slowly into the pond. The water will press the plastic tightly into the excavation. Wait two or three days after the pond has filled up before you fix the edges with flat rocks (see Shaping the Pond's Edge, on page 15).

Drainpipe: The drainpipe is installed in the same way as it is in a concrete pond, but it has to be carefully welded to the plastic before the water is run into the pond.

Shaping the Pond's Edge

To make the pond look more natural in its setting, the edges, except for the flat sections where the ducks climb in and out, are coverd with natural stones. Pieces of slate, flags of limestone, or plain, flat rocks work well. If your pond is built of concrete, such rocks can be set into the top of the walls. With plastic ponds, they are laid on the protruding rim of plastic.

Planting the Pond and Its Surroundings

A new keeper of ornamental ducks is often eager to recreate a natural habitat by planting marsh and water plants in and around his duck pond. But if you think you can transform your pond into a natural-looking landscape complete with water lilies, reeds, rushes, frogs, fish, and turtles, you are in for an unpleasant surprise. A duck has only one thing on its mind, and that is to search for food as assiduously as possible. A charmingly planted garden pond with just one pair of ducks on it will soon lose its aesthetic appeal. Torn-off leaves and water-lily blossoms will soon be floating on the water's surface, the frogs will disappear, the fish will retreat to hidden corners, and the water turtles' quiet way of life will be disrupted.

Still, it is possible to have a decorative green plant cover on the water by planting duckweed. This plant will thrive, though you may have to add a few bucketfuls from time to time. And you can also incorporate some shrubbery and green grass into the surrounding landscape. But flowering perennials and flower beds should always be protected from the voracious appetite of the ducks by a low chicken-wire fence.

Plants for the Duck Run: Some indestructible plants that can be planted to provide greenery in place of a lawn are ground ivy (*Glechomá hederacea*), silverweed (*Potentilla anserina*), various camomile species (*Matricaria*), and for a larger plant, the large-leafed butterbur (*Petasites*).

Plants for the Edge of the Pond: Some taller flowering plants and decorative grasses that ducks don't eat are day lilies (*Hemerocallis*), yellow iris (*Iris pseudacorus*), Arundinaria bamboo plants, the tall perennial grass eulalia (*Miscanthus*), and in milder climates, the magnificent pampas grass (*Cotaderia*).

Ornamental ducks like to build their nests in the dense foliage of stinging nettle, butterbur, and smartweed.

Protection from Wind and Sun: Low-growing conifers, such as Chinese juniper (*Juniperus chinensis pfitzneriana*) and dwarf pine (*Pinus mugo pumilio*), serve this function well. Ducks don't nibble on them but use their shade to rest in and find hidden places among them for building their nests.

When you visit duck breeders and zoological gardens, examine their duck areas and take a close look at the shrubs and bushes growing near the duck ponds. Any plants that thrive there are likely to do well in or around your pond.

A Natural Duck Pond

Natural ponds are excellent for ornamental as well as for commercial ducks if they are not polluted by household sewage or industrial effluents. Check the water quality carefully before releasing ducks into the pond because polluted water can poison them. If you find fish, no matter what kind, swimming around actively, this is a good indication that the water is suitable for ducks as well. To keep the ducks from escaping, the pond and the area around it should be enclosed with a wire-mesh fence.

Carp ponds have proven ideal for keeping utility ducks. The fast-growing and productive Pekin ducks can be kept this way. A side benefit is that their dung fertilizes the pond organically, which leads to rapid plankton growth. The plankton means that the carp have more food and therefore grow faster. The maximum number of ducks that should be kept on a 1-acre area of water is about 100.

Keeping ornamental ducks on larger ponds or on park waters with natural vegetation is ideal in theory. But you have to be braced for losses caused by foxes, martens, dogs, and cats because ornamental ducks, to keep them from flying away, have to have their wings clipped (see Rendering Ducks Flightless, page 34). Small species, such as green-winged teal, garganey, and Baikal teal, cannot be kept at all on waters in such unsurveyable terrain because they would soon wander off, never to be seen again.

There are also problems when the water begins to freeze. That is why at some point in the fall ornamental ducks should get used to eating in a wire cage with a door that can be raised and lowered (see drawing opposite). They get used to it quite quickly. Then, when the water first begins to ice over, you close the door while the ducks are eating. It is easy to take them out of the cage and move them to a barn with an attached aviary, where they spend the winter. Many parks use this method to winter over their swans.

Keeping ducks is usually not permitted on the waters of fish hatcheries and spawning grounds or in protected wildlife areas. The reason for this is that ducks like to eat fish eggs and fry. In protected wildlife areas they also threaten tadpoles, rare aquatic plants, and the eggs of amphibians.

Other places that are unsuitable are standing bodies of water without inlets or outlets and small, dirty puddles. In such waters, lack of oxygen often leads to decomposition processes during hot, dry summers, and ducks may die of botulism poisoning (see Botulism, page 43).

The Duck Shelter

Both ornamental and commercial ducks require shelter from the cold of winter. On sunny winter days, ducks should be let outside. Since they are fed inside the shelter they will return there in the evening of their own accord. On farms, utility ducks are frequently housed in such places as empty chicken coops or pigpens.

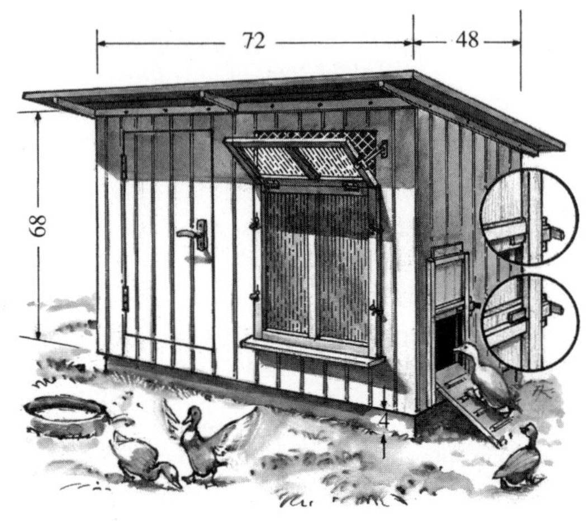

A duck shelter offers ornamental or utility ducks protection when it is too cold. A little door on the right can be used by the ducks to get outside in good weather. The inset drawings show the lock on the door frame keeping the door up (above) and locking it shut when it is down (below).

Building Ordinances

Before you start building your duck shelter, you should check to be sure that your plans conform to any local building ordinances that may be in effect. As a general rule, all permanent structures, regardless of size, have to be approved. It is therefore a good idea to call the local authorities to tell them of your plans. If you want to build on leased land, you will first have to ask the landowner's permission.

A family of ringed teal on an artificial pond. On the left is the female with her ducklings; the drake is on the right.

Housing and Environment

Method of Construction and Size

A shelter for ornamental and/or commercial ducks is usually built of wood and is, for practical reasons, supported by a foundation of cinderblocks or concrete. This is the only way to protect the wood from the moisture in the ground and thus to keep it from rotting. A foundation also makes it harder for rats and predators, such as fox and marten, to penetrate into the shelter. The shelter is sited in such a way that the inside gets as much light as possible, which means that the front should face south or southeast.

The size of the shelter depends primarily on the desires and constraints of the owner. A space 6 feet wide, 4 feet deep, and 5 feet 8 inches high (2 × 1.2 × 1.7 m) is sufficient to accommodate one or two pairs of ducks. The foundation should extend 20 inches (50 cm) down into the ground and rise 4 inches (10 cm) above it. The walls are built with boards on both sides of the studs and insulated with styrofoam. The structure is usually covered with a shed roof that slopes down toward the back. It should extend somewhat more over the front of the building than over the sides to keep the rain out.

Floor and Bedding

The floor of the shelter should consist of a 5- to 6 inch (12–15 cm) layer of broken brick or gravel, onto which 2½ to 3 inches (6–8 cm) of concrete is poured and smoothed. Such a concrete floor is easy to clean and disinfect. Then a thick layer of sand, peat moss, or sawdust is put down to serve as bedding. When the bedding gets dirty it is easy to clean out. If it is very cold, a layer of straw should be put on top.

Some ornamental ducks:
Above, left: red-crested pochard drake; Above, right: red-crested pochard female; below: a pair of mandarin ducks.

Temperature

Most ornamental and all commercial ducks are quite hardy and are not bothered if the temperature drops a few degrees below freezing. After all, they are equipped with a warm, thick down coat. Tropical ducks sometimes freeze their toes and webs when it gets very cold. To keep the shelter warm enough, you can install a heat lamp on the ceiling.

Windows and Doors

To let in as much light as possible, the shelter should have a large window with the kind of glass used in gardening for cold frames. The inside walls should be whitewashed every year. A door next to the window connects the shelter to the run and pond or to the aviary. A second door is useful so that the caretaker doesn't have to walk through the outdoor run or aviary every time the ducks need to be fed or their house cleaned.

Food and Water Dishes; Swimming Basin

Ducks have a habit of softening the food they are about to eat by dipping their full bill into the drinking water. This means, of course, that the floor soon gets very messy. To minimize the mess, food and water dishes are set on a rack mounted on a low platform.

It is important, especially for diving ducks, that they have a place to swim even inside the shelter. A galvanized tub can serve for this purpose. It can be sunk into the floor or made accessible for the ducks by means of a small ladder. The dirty water can be drained to the outside, where the ground can absorb it. It is often necessary to change the water every day.

A Large Duck House

If you plan to breed ducks or raise ducks for the market, you will need a larger setup. The duck house described here as an example is adequate for a maximum of 40 breeding ducks or 80 ducklings to be raised for market.

Construction Plan

The structure described here is 13 feet, 1 inch (4 m) wide and 16 feet, 5 inches (5 m) long and rests on a cinderblock or concrete foundation. The floor is prepared the same way as for a small shelter (see page 19). The wooden side walls are 40 inches (1 m) high, and the ridge of the gable roof is 75 inches (1.9 m) off the floor. There are two windows 40 inches (1 m) wide and 20 inches (.5 m) high in each side wall and four small doors just above ground level with openings 10 × 10 inches (25 × 25 cm) leading into the outdoor runs.

On the gable end facing away from the prevailing wind, there is a 70 × 35 inch (180 by 90-cm) door, and a walkway 35 inches (90 cm) wide leading down the middle of the building. Feeding and watering the birds, as well as cleaning the four compartments on each side is easily done from this center walkway. Each compartment is 6 feet, 5 inches (2 m) long and 3 feet, 2½ inches (1 m) wide and can accommodate one breeding unit of commercial ducks consisting of one drake and four hens.

Fattening Ducks: If you want to raise ducks for market, you will want to take down the low (24 inches or 60 cm) wooden walls that separate the compartments. Now you have an area of 172 square feet (16 m²) available for your ducks. The standard space requirement for 20 baby ducklings is about 11 square feet (1 m²) during the first two weeks. During the third to fifth week the same space will be adequate for only 8 to 10 ducklings, and from the sixth to the eighth week only 4 to 5 birds can be contained in that space.

Food and Water

Feeders and waterers (see page 24) are located on the wall bordering the walkway and should be placed on a wire-covered platform. This is to reduce soaking of the bedding as much as possible. Ducks like to spill water. A drainage channel that runs through all the compartments along the walkway is a useful feature. Small gates in the wall along the walkway provide access to the compartments for cleaning.

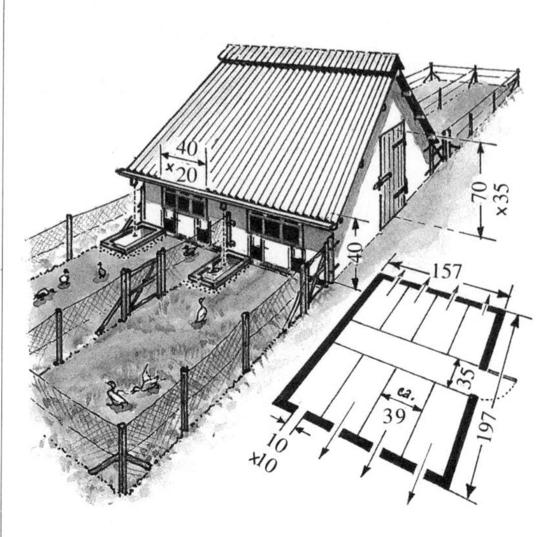

A duck house that can be used for raising 40 to 80 ducks for market. Breeding ducks should spend only the night indoors and go outside during the day except during cold winter weather.

Temperature

The temperature in the duck quarters should not rise above 77° F (25°C) in the summer, and it should not drop below freezing in the winter. Air humidity should not be too high because high humidity slows down the egg-laying. That is why there should be air vents at the ridge of the roof to insure adequate ventilation.

Outdoor Runs

Ducks should stay indoors only at night and when the weather is very cold; the rest of the time they should be out. Each compartment is therefore connected to a run the birds can get to through a small door. The runs are separated from each other by a 16-inch (40-cm) chickenwire fence. There should be a water channel, made of concrete, 32 inches wide by 16 inches deep (80 cm wide × 40 cm deep) running through all the runs at the far end from the duck house to give the ducks a chance to swim.

An Aviary for Ducks

An aviary is a space for birds that is enclosed on all sides, including the top, with grating or wire mesh, and that is large enough for the occupants to use their wings for flying. Usually only ornamental ducks are kept in aviaries. For small species the aviary provides safety from predators, and many ornamental ducks can be purebred only in aviaries because they are likely to hybridize otherwise.

Construction

An aviary should always be situated so that it gets sunshine at least part of the day. It also has to keep out predators. Digging the wire mesh into the ground a couple of inches is not enough to keep out foxes and martens, which can dig under the wire. An aviary, just like a duck shelter (see page 19), should have a foundation made of cinderblocks or concrete. It should be 16 inches (40 cm) thick, be dug 20 inches (50 cm) into the ground, and rise 12 inches (30 cm) above the ground.

Wire Mesh: The wire mesh is held up by metal posts that are set into the concrete. Instead of posts you can use metal brackets with U-shaped clamps into which wooden posts can be fitted and fastened with screws.

Use a fine wire mesh intended for use with chicks. The gaps in the weave should be ½ inch (1.25 cm) or no more than ¾ inch (2 cm), small enough to keep even sparrows out. Hardware cloth, which is made of wires welded into squares, looks very attractive. The wire mesh forming the ceiling should not be stretched too tight but should sag slightly. This way it will give a little if you have ducks that can fly and bump into it in their steep take-off pattern.

Floor: The aviary floor should include a swimming basin (see An Artificial Duck Pond, page 13). Because ducks carry quite a lot of water with them when they leave the swimming basin, the surrounding floor has to have good drainage. Otherwise the bottom of the aviary will soon turn into a bog of wet mud. When you build the aviary, dig down 20 inches (50 cm) and fill the excavation with a layer of coarse gravel, one of fine gravel, and a top layer of sand.

Decorating

Any aviary looks more attractive if it is landscaped. A log placed horizontally behind the swimming basin and a few erratic boulders of various sizes arranged in a natural pattern enhance the looks of an aviary. Trying to incorporate greenery into an aviary inhabited by ducks is often a vain enterprise. Ornamental ducks confined to a small area tend to ravage plants. But don't give up too quickly. Try a few different kinds of plants (see Planting the Pond and Its Surroundings, page 15). Nest sites are set up in the back of the aviary (see page 48). For ducks like the wood duck and the mandarin duck, which like to nest in tree holes, these sites should be located at least 20 inches (50 cm) above the ground and made accessible for the birds by way of a slanted log or a small ladder.

Diet

Like chickens, ducks are omnivorous. But because their senses of taste and smell are more discriminating, they are more particular than chickens about what they eat. Their nutritional requirements also vary depending on their stage of development and on the changing seasons of the year. An organism that is still growing needs different food from one that has reached sexual maturity and may be producing eggs. All this has to be taken into account if ducks are to be fed properly.

Digestion

To get a better idea of what ducks should eat, you should first familiarize yourself with a duck's alimentary canal and how it functions.

Food Intake: The bill and the tongue serve to pick up food, which is lubricated by secretions from the salivary glands on the inside of the bill and on the tongue so that it can slide down the gullet or esophagus. A widening in the esophagus at the lower end has a function similar to that of a chicken's crop, namely to regulate how much food enters the stomach at any one time. The food that is swallowed collects at the bottom of the gullet and is then passed on in small portions to the proventriculus, the glandular or true stomach of a bird. The lining of the proventriculus is covered with glands that produce thick mucus and gastric juices containing hydrochloric acid and pepsin, substances that break down protein. Beneath the lining there is a thick layer of muscles which propel the food to the gizzard by means of rhythmic contractions.

Grinding the Food Down: The walls of the gizzard, too, are made up of a thick layer of muscle and a lining containing glands. The secretion of these glands hardens on the inner surface of the gizzard, forming two plates that rub against each other. Every 20 seconds, the walls of the gizzard contract, pressing the two plates together. Since ducks also swallow grains of quartz sand, or grit (see page 26), all the hard components of the food are crushed. This mechanical rubbing action is a kind of substitute for teeth.

Absorbing Nutrients: The food that has thus been "masticated" then goes through a passage from the gizzard into the duodenum. The pancreas and the bile ducts open into the small intestine, contributing secretions that continue the digestive process of the food pulp. Nutrients that are broken down into chemical elements that can be assimilated by the organism are then absorbed through the intestinal lining and enter the bloodstream. A similar process goes on in the large intestine. The caeca, two long, blind tubes similar to our appendix, branch off from the large intestine. Their main function is to produce bacteria which break down cellulose, thus releasing its food value in a form usable by the organism.

The large intestine widens toward the posterior end and forms a roundish chamber, the cloaca. As in all other birds, not only the alimentary canal but the urinary and reproductive canals as well empty into the cloaca.

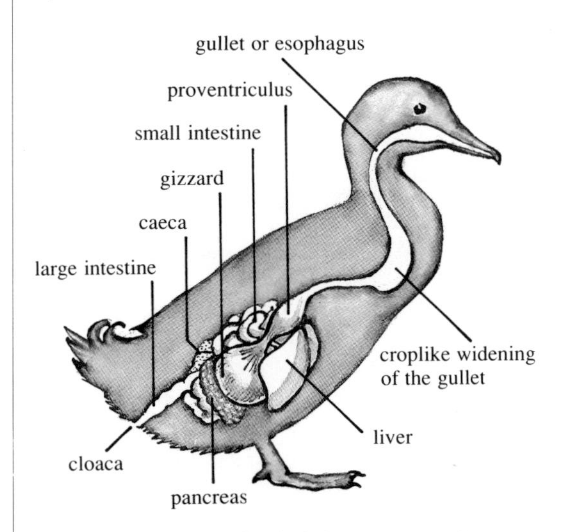

The internal organs of a duck. Ducks are omnivorous. They have digestive organs that grind up even hard foods.

Foods

The preceding overview of the digestive system of ducks should be of some help in deciding on the makeup of your ducks' diet. Ducks eat food that comes from two sources: vegetable and animal.

Foods from Vegetable Sources

The various cereal grains are one of the most important food items for commercial as well as ornamental ducks. The food value of grain consists of carbohydrates and proteins in the endosperm (the part of the kernel that is used to make white flour), and the fats in the germ. All these nutrients are easily digestible and are present in varying amounts in all grains.

Ducks eat grain in the following order of preference: corn, wheat, barley, oats, and rye. To make sure that the birds don't just pick out one kind and leave the rest, you should mix and coarsely grind a combination of grains.

Corn is especially high in carbohydrates and fats. This makes corn a good feed for ducks that are raised for market. But to prevent it from affecting the color and taste of the meat, it should never make up more than 12% to 15% of the diet. In the winter months corn is also good for ornamental ducks that spend some time on the water. Smaller species can eat corn only if is cracked.

Wheat, which contains 12.3% of raw protein, is the most protein-rich grain. It plays a very important role in the diet of ducks both as a supplement to other feeds and as a component in commercial mixed feeds. But if ducks are given too much wheat, the protein/carbohydrate balance in their diet may get upset and the food will not be used optimally.

Barley is not very popular with ducks or with other poultry because the grains are pointed and hard. That is why it is usually coarsely ground and fed in the form of groats. Since barley has a positive effect on meat production as well as on the quality of the meat, it should always form part of the diet of ducks that are raised for market.

Unhulled oats are high in indigestible substances—fiber accounts for almost 10%—and are therefore not as rich in nutrients as other grains. But the roughage is important for proper digestion. Oats have a generally beneficial effect on all kinds of bodily processes, as is demonstrated by the fact that rolled oats are fed to young chicks of all the members of the poultry family. It has also been asserted that oat hulls in the diet discourage feather-eating (see page 42). Oat hulls also result in better breeding results, which is why oats should always be included in the diet of breeding ducks.

Sprouted oats are often given to ducks in the winter months when there is little green food available for them.

Rye, even though most ducks are not fond of it, is an excellent feed grain. Their dislike is based not so much on taste as on the pointed shape of the kernels. It is best, therefore, to feed the birds ground rye in a meal mixture.

Millet is available commercially in several varieties that differ considerably from each other in appearance as well as in nutritional value.

Milo, because of its high protein content, deserves to be singled out. It is a sorghum that comes originally from Africa but is now grown extensively in America. Milo is an excellent feed grain that can be given whole. It is often one of the ingredients in commercial feed mixes.

Spray millet is not recommended for baby ducklings. Because of the hard seed coat very little of the food value can be absorbed by the digestive system of very young chicks. Hulled millet (which, however, is quite expensive) can be fed to the baby ducklings of fancy ornamental breeds.

Middlings are a byproduct of grain milling. When flour is produced, the outer cellulose walls of the kernels as well as bits of the sticky layers underneath, which are high in protein, are removed. Middlings are therefore a highly valuable animal feed. They are often mixed with boiled potatoes for feeding ducks..

Stale bread is often given to ornamental as well as to commercial ducks. It is high in carbohydrates and easily digested by the birds. Sometimes it is mixed with commercial feeds to complement the protein. Stale bread is softened in liquid before it is fed to ducks.

Hemp seed is often given to small species of ornamental ducks. Hemp seed is high in fats and lends gloss to the plumage.

Acorns are high in carbohydrates. They are fed whole and unpeeled to dabbling ducks, that is, ducks that gather food in shallow water. These ducks are very fond of acorns.

Potatoes, among the root vegetables, probably play the most important role in the diet of ducks. Ducks like potatoes which must, however, be cooked and given in combination with proportionate amounts of protein foods since potatoes are almost pure starch. If the potatoes have started sprouting during storage, the sprouting eyes must be cut out because the shoots contain solanin, which is poisonous. Potatoes are generally combined with meal to form a moist mash of crumbly consistency.

Sugar beets are chopped and steamed for feeding to ducks. Where market ducks are being raised on soft foods, sugar beets are frequently substituted for potatoes.

Carrots are also a nutritious food. Because they are so high in carotene they are often added to the diet of baby ducklings. They can be given steamed, chopped, or grated and mixed into the soft food.

Greens are eaten enthusiastically. Nothing will make your utility or ornamental ducks happier than to let them graze on a meadow. Grass does not have much food value, but it does contain vitamins and trace elements, and it provides roughage, which is essential for the digestive process. Feed grass and other greens before they flower because, as the plants age, the proportion of crude fiber in them increases, making them harder to digest. If you give your ducks cut grass, you also have to watch out that the grass stems are not too long. If long stems are swallowed whole, they may compact into balls in the lower, sack-like part of the gullet and cause a blockage that may be fatal. Young nettles, dandelions, yarrow, and chickweed are some herbaceous plants that can be chopped fine and added to soft food; they are eaten happily in this form by baby ducklings.

Duckweeds (Lemna), as the name implies, are popular with ducks. These small, free-floating aquatic plants always harbor innumerable small organisms that form an almost indispensible part of the rearing foods for the chicks of ornamental ducks. Duckweeds have to be very fresh when fed to ducks. Pour them from a bucket into the ducks' water basin and let the birds sift them out.

Feeders and waterers should be placed near each other because ducks have the habit of dunking each billful of food into water to soften it.

If there are no greens at all available for your ducks in the winter, you may want to mix some finely chopped lettuce into their food occasionally.

Foods from Animal Sources

Protein from animal sources is absolutely essential in the diet of ducks and is available in abun-

Dabbling ducks, like the common mallard, forage for food both in the water and on land. When bottom-feeding, they upend, submerging the head and the front of the body with the rear end sticking up in the air.

dance in many commerical feeds.

Blood meal is probably the most protein-rich food. A good brand contains as much as 86 to 89% protein. However, blood meal often has acids added to it and in this form is not well suited to ducks.

Fish meal is made of whole fish and fish by-products and is manufactured by fish-processing plants. It contains proteins that are essential in the diet of ducks. However, the finishing rations given to ducks before slaughter should include only meal from high-quality, low-fat fish, such as cod, that leaves no trace of fish smell or taste in the meat. The crucial difference between various fish meals is their fat content, which also determines the price. If the fat content is high, the fish meal may get rancid if not used soon enough. By the way, none of the good commercial poultry feeds relies exclusively on fish meal for protein; some of the protein is always supplied by meat meal.

Meat meal comes from the meat industry and is made up of meat by-products that are unusable for human consumption. It is a good protein supplement for mixed feeds. There is also a meat meal that comes from the cadavers of domestic animals that have died of natural causes. This meat is processed in accordance with health regulations that ensure that no diseases will be transmitted by it, and it can therefore be used as feed without worry.

Dried shrimp and shrimp meal contain 59% protein. These are often mixed into the soft food of ornamental ducks, but they have to be soaked first because they are hard as a rock when dry.

Milk products, with their easily digestible protein, also make good duck food. They can be fed in the form of cottage cheese, skim milk, buttermilk, or whey. Fresh pot or cottage cheese—which must, however, be dry—has been successfully used as an easily digestible component in the first food eaten by baby ducklings (see Feeding Baby Ducklings, page 28). Skim milk and buttermilk are often mixed into the soft food given to ducks raised for market. Milk should be fed to ducks after it has soured and coagulated. Nonfat powdered milk and dried whey are also a good source of protein and vitamins.

Diving ducks, like the tufted duck, which is now quite common in Europe, and find their food almost exclusively by diving to the bottom of the water and searching for mussels, clams, snails, and worms.

Food Supplements

Among these are grit, calcium in the form of phosphate or carbonate of lime, and vitamins.

Grit is a mixture of small grains of quartz and calcareous spar. It is used by the ducks to grind down hard food particles in the gizzard (see Digestion, page 22). Ducks always have to have access to this necessary grit.

Phosphate of lime is sold commercially as "food lime" and is made from bones.

Carbonic lime consists of ground seashells. Female birds have an increased need for calcium during laying season because every new eggshell they manufacture depletes their own body of calcium (see Egg Formation and Egg Laying, page 60).

Vitamins are usually present in sufficient quantities in natural ingredients. The commercially available feeds that supply a complete diet (see next column) also contain all the necessary vitamins in sufficient amounts.

Since commercially available mixes are made up of the ingredients already discussed above, it seems appropriate to include them here.

Feed meals, also called dry rations or mash, are mixtures of ingredients designed to meet the nutritional needs of ducks at various times of year and at different stages of life. Thus you can buy commercial rations for baby ducklings, for young ducks, for laying birds, and for market ducks.

The term "meal" does not imply that the product consists entirely of cereal meals. On the contrary, the feed probably includes ingredients like blood meal, fish and meat meal, all of which are proteins of animal origin. If such a feed contains all the essential nutrients as established by scientific research, it can be be used as the sole food for the ducks.

Never give ducks dry meal. Their broad bills are not designed for picking up and holding flour or farinaceous substances, and much will be spilled. Mix meals with just enough water to hold them together in a crumbly consistency; do not make a soupy mixture.

Complete Rations and Feeds

Complete rations are scientifically composed feed mixtures that contain all the essential nutrients, including vitamins and trace elements. These rations are sold in the form of meals and of pellets. Using them not only simplifies keeping ducks for the beginner but also helps prevent major feeding mistakes.

Pellet feeds are made of mealy mixed with sticky substances like molasses or cod-liver oil and subjected to high pressure to make them cohere in pellet form. These nutritionally complete pellet feeds are used almost exclusively in large operations because this feeding method is very simple and therefore economical.

Grains like barley and rye, which are very healthy but are not eaten enthusiastically by ducks because of their hardness and pointed shape, are readily consumed in pellet form. When you buy pellet feed, check the size of the pellets: Young ducklings should get smaller pellets, older ducks, larger ones. There are two drawbacks to relying on pellet feeds: Pellets are more expensive than other forms of feed, and if the birds live under crowded conditions (as when raised for market), pellet feeds aggravate the tendency of ducks to feather eating (see page 42).

Commercial feed mixes for poultry generally come in the form of mixed grains, feeds for rearing chicks and for layers, as well as in the form of nutritionally complete rations, either as pellets or as loose meals.

Concentrated protein is a commercially manufactured mixture of animal proteins (fish, blood, and meat meals and powdered milk) and/or vegetable proteins (corn gluten, oil cake, brewer's yeast) that has concentrated vitamins and minerals added to it. To make up for the low-protein content of carbohydrate foods, such as potatoes, about 15 to 20% of a concentrated protein ration should be added to them so that the right carbohydrate/protein balance is achieved.

Soft food is a mixture of food items in a moist

but not wet form, such as boiled potatoes with cereal meals and chopped greens.

Where to Buy Duck Feed

Many feed stores carry a varied assortment of feeds suitable for ducks. You can also look for advertisements in poultry magazines to find out what duck feeds are available, or duck breeders will be happy to tell you what their experience with various feeds has been and give you the names and addresses of their suppliers.

Storing Feeds

Grains, pellets, and meals should be packed in paper or plastic sacks and stored in dry, airy rooms. They keep fresh only if they are stored in this way. Every couple of weeks, check all the feed you have stored for signs of vermin. Grain beetles, various moths, mice, and rats can quickly become established if you don't watch out. Make sure the animal feed you store is easy to survey. Moldy feed must never be fed to ducks. Soft food always has to be fresh; never mix more than your ducks will eat in one day because it spoils quickly in warm weather and then is unfit for consumption.

Feeding

Whether you keep ornamental or utility ducks, you will want to feed them optimally to keep them in the best possible health.

There are two feeding methods: You can give your ducks a nutritionally complete ration, or you can feed them a combination of different foods. The results of the two methods are the same.

Feeding a Complete Ration

The feed industry produces nutritionally complete rations (see page 26) in the form of meals and of pellets of various sizes. These rations can be given to the animals without any additional foods. Large-scale duck operations, where tens of thousands of ducks are raised for market, rely entirely on these feeds for economic reasons. If you don't want to be bothered mixing your ducks' food yourself because you lack the time or because you simply don't feel like doing it, you may want to use the commercial rations even though you have a comparatively small flock. The commercial, nutritionally complete rations could be called feeds for lazy farmers because all you need to do is to pour the feed into the food hoppers or troughs.

Many owners of ducks who would rather feed their table scraps and vegetable trimmings to their animals than throw them in the garbage and who don't mind spending half an hour mixing their ducks' food will find the second feeding method just right for them.

Feeding a Mixed Diet

To make sure your ducks eat enough of the food you prepare for them, you have to make it appealing and make sure their bills can cope with it. This means that everything is cut to the proper size and that wholesome but less savory items are mixed in with the more palatable ones.

Grains should be cracked; greens, chopped fine; fruits, cut into pieces; and boiled potatoes, mashed. Greens and grass have to be given very fresh, on the same day they are cut.

All these ingredients are mixed together so that the resulting mash is moist but not soggy or runny. It's not as hard to achieve this consistency as it may sound: Just keep stirring liquid (water, skim milk, or whey) into the food until it is moist enough to stick together. If by mistake you add too much liquid and the food gets soupy, just add some dry items, such as stale bread.

You should not give ducks runny foods because it is harder for them to pick it up with their broad bills than food that is solid enough to stick together.

The ducks also get wet food all over their heads and the rest of their feathers, and what gets spilled is stepped on and spread all around the food trough.

Feeding Utility Ducks

Ducks shouldn't get the same food all the time because the nutritional requirements of their organisms change with age and with the different phases of the life cycle. The body of a fast-growing duckling has different needs from that of a laying duck.

The composition of a diet for utility ducks should be somewhat different for each of the following stages: baby ducklings, young adult birds, market birds, breeding ducks during laying season, and breeding ducks during the rest period between breeding cycles.

Feeding Baby Ducklings

When baby ducklings hatch they have enough food stored in the yolk sack to last them for the first two or three days. That is why they are not fed for the first 24 hours after hatching.

How Often to Feed: During the first weeks baby ducklings should be fed six or seven times a day at roughly equal intervals. The number of meals can be reduced to between three and five in the course of the second to the eighth week. During weeks eight to twelve, three meals are sufficient.

How Much to Feed: It is hard to say just how much food a baby duckling consumes a day because some ducklings are very active eaters while others are exceptionally modest in their food consumption. But even beginners have no problem telling how much they should give their ducklings to eat. When all the food is eaten up between meals, it is time to increase the ration. Keep increasing the amount until some food is left over, which is a clear sign that the birds have had enough to eat. Breeders sometimes call this "feeding to satiation."

During the first three weeks you can feed the ducklings exclusively on a nutritionally complete commercial duckling ration that contains 18% protein and is made up of pellets ⅛ inch (3 mm) in diameter. Be sure to place a shallow dish with drinking water next to the feeder.

However, instead of using the commercial ration, you can compose your own. Combine 40 parts oat flakes, 40 parts cracked barley for chicks, 20 parts bran, and some finely chopped greens and slowly add water while stirring constantly until the mixture is moist but still crumbly. This food can be given to the ducklings from the first through the

Mallard duck

Shoveler

Shoveler in the act of feeding

A duck's bill is a highly specialized tool. Equipped with extremely sensitive tactile organs, it easily detects small organisms and sieves them out of the mud and water.

seventh day. From the eighth through the twenty-seventh day they should get a soft food made of 60 parts cracked cereals (corn, oats, barley), 15 parts protein foods (soured milk or cottage cheese), and 25 parts greens. From the fourth week on you can give them a mixture of 25 parts boiled and mashed potatoes, 35 parts cracked cereals, 15 parts protein foods, and 25 parts greens.

In addition to the these mixed foods, the ducklings should have grit and calcium (see page 26) in separate dishes.

Feeding Market Ducks

Rations for market ducks are designed to produce the greatest weight gain within the shortest period of time while using as little feed as possible. In the method that is now used universally to produce market ducklings—which attain a weight of 5 ½ pounds (2.5 kg) by the time they are eight or nine weeks old—the birds are fed rations for fast growth from the day they are hatched. During these eight or nine weeks the ducklings multiply their birth weight by 50 at an average consumption of feed of 20 to 22 pounds (9–10 kg). It is hardly surprising that such dramatic growth requires a diet high in protein. Using a commercial, nutritionally complete ration takes the least amount of effort and reduces waste of food to a minimum.

Complete Ration for Baby Ducklings: During their first three weeks of life, ducklings raised for market receive a ration with an 18% protein content and a pellet size of ⅛ inch (2.5 mm).

Complete ration for market ducks: From the fourth week on, the birds are given a ration with 16% protein and a pellet size of 3/16 inch (4.5 mm), and this diet is maintained until the ducks are ready for slaughter at eight or nine weeks.

Both of these feeds are also available in the form of meals or mash.

Fattening Ducks on Potatoes: Especially on farms, potatoes are still used to fatten ducks. The potatoes, which contain very little protein, have to be fortified with a mixture of cracked grains and a protein concentrate (see page 26). For best weight gain, a proportion of 65% mashed potatoes to 35% mixed protein food is recommended. This food is readily eaten by the ducks and can be made even more appealing by adding some skim milk. It is given three times a day in sufficient amounts so that after the ducks have eaten their fill, there is still a little left over for the next few hours—however, the food should be all gone by the next scheduled feeding.

The total amount eaten during nine weeks of feeding is about 33 to 44 pounds (15–20 kg) of potatoes and about 11 pounds (5 kg) of mixed protein food per bird.

Ducklings raised for market are not provided with a swimming basin, but for them to be able to keep their plumage clean they have to be able to take baths several times a week.

Feeding Laying Ducks

Ducklings destined to be layers are fed on the same regimen for the first seven weeks as those raised for market (see Feeding Baby Ducklings, page 28). From the eighth through the thirteenth week, the time when they undergo the juvenile molt, the future laying ducks need a 14% protein diet. A nutritionally complete ration for young hens that has a protein content of 14% is generally used for this period.

Utility ducks become sexually active when they are five to seven months old. Lightweight breeds, like Indian runners and Campbells, start laying eggs as early as five to six months; heavyweight types like the Pekin, Aylesbury, and Rouen ducks mature later and don't start laying until seven months.

Single ration: About two to four weeks before the ducks are expected to start laying, they are shifted over to a ration for breeding birds. The simplest method is to give them a nutritionally complete, 16%-protein ration for laying hens.

Mixed food: If there is no appropriate commercial ration available, laying ducks can be given 80% cracked grains and 20% meat or fish meal.

If you want to use potatoes for your laying ducks, you should combine 25% mashed potatoes, 10% cracked corn, 10% cracked rye, 10% wheat middlings, 10% fish meal, 10% meat meal, and 25% mixed grains composed of corn, oats, and barley.

Another alternative is to compose a feed of 70% potatoes, 8% chopped sugar beets, 7% wheat middlings, 5% cracked corn and oats, and 10% meat meal.

Foraging on land. The wigeon belongs to those ducks that wander around like sheep, cropping young grass and tender leaves.

Feeding During the Rest Period

When the breeding ducks stop laying, which is usually in the fall, they are put on a "maintenance" diet. This diet contains fewer calories than the laying mash the birds have been eating because the hormonal activities of the organism should slow down until the next laying season starts. If you kept on feeding the birds a laying diet, they would continue producing eggs, though at longer intervals, until physically exhausted. The maintenance diet is supposed to keep the birds in good condition but without letting them get fat or stimulating any sexual drives. For this purpose a nutritionally complete, 14%-protein ration for young hens has been used with good results.

Feeding Ornamental Ducks

There are no special, nutritionally complete rations on the market for ornamental ducks. These birds are given the same kinds of food as utility ducks, except that no rations designed for raising market ducks are used. Trying to adjust the feed to the age of the birds and to the seasons works only if the ducks are kept in an aviary or on a small backyard pond. If they live in larger enclosures on more extensive bodies of water, attempts to control their diet are pointless.

Most people who keep ducks in such a setting have more than one species, and the birds are of different ages and follow different breeding calendars. Wild birds are bound to show up at the feeding stations and will consume a considerable share of the special food you put out for your ducks. You will have to put food out several times a day to make sure your ornamental birds do not go hungry. Under such conditions all you can do is supply an adequate all-purpose diet that stays the same all year. But if you keep ornamental ducks in an aviary or on a pond in an enclosure in your backyard, I recommend the following:

Baby Ducklings: A nutritionally complete ration in the form of a mash containing 16% protein should be given for the first three weeks. In the first week, to get them interested in eating, you should add finely chopped, hard-boiled egg yolk and enough water for the feed to be moist but still crumbly. Sprinkle finely chopped greens over the top and, if possible, put a shallow dish full of water and duckweed next to the mixed food.

The little ducklings need to be fed six or seven times a day at regular intervals for the first two weeks. Feed them to satiation, that is, just as much as they will consume at feeding time. Always remove the leftovers because they spoil quickly.

When the ducklings are three weeks old they can start eating small seeds like silver millet, birdseed mixtures for canaries and/or parakeets, and finely cracked wheat in addition to the ration they have been getting all along.The seeds should be sprinkled into a shallow dish with water, where the ducklings will gobble them up. Be sure to always have grit and sand available.

Starting with the fourth or fifth week, the ducklings should gradually be shifted over from a diet for baby ducklings to one for adult birds. You make this transition by mixing a little more of the new food into the accustomed fare every day.

Mature Birds: I recommend using soft food made up of 30% mashed potatoes, 10% wheat middlings, 20% cracked barley, 20% chopped, dry shrimp, 15% bread, and 5% crushed seashells. Add whatever greens are in season, finely chopped.

Laying Birds: In an aviary or on a garden pond, a nutritionally complete, 16%-protein ration for laying hens can be recommended. Use the pellet form. Start giving it one month before the laying season of the particular species of ornamental or wild duck that you have begins (see Ornamental Ducks and Utility Ducks, page 34).

During the *rest period*, ornamental ducks can be given a nutritionally complete 14% protein ration designed for young hens.

A Duck Pasture

If you have a fairly large area of lawn or meadow, you should let your domestic ducks loose on it. They will busily comb the area for snails, slugs, caterpillars, grubs, and worms. They keep the grass down at the same time, being especially fond of the tender, small leaves of plants. Ducks like nettle shoots, dandelion greens, yarrow, orache, chicory, and chickweed. After the ducks are through grazing, the grass growing back will look healthy and dark green. The ducks have not only kept the grass short but also fertilized the lawn.

There seems to be no need to worry about ducks eating poisonous plants; I'm not aware of a single instance of ducks getting sick from eating poisonous plants when grazing. In the evening offer your ducks a handful of grain each in their quarters.

Care and Maintenance

Quarantine

It would be a serious mistake to place newly acquired ducks in a yard where other waterfowl are already living. First of all, there is the possibility that the newcomers, which are still unsure of themselves and timid, would be persecuted and possibly killed by the already established birds. But there is an even greater danger: The new birds might introduce a disease into a previously healthy flock. That is why new birds have to be quarantined for at least a week or, if there is any reason to be suspicious, longer. This means that you have to have a separate space, apart from the main duckyard, to house new birds for an observation period. In the winter you can use an empty shed (see The Duck Shelter, page 16). If the ducks turn out to be sick, the shed can be easily disinfected.

Proper Acclimation

If the new ducks pass the quarantine period with flying colors and you want to let them join the other occupants of a pond, you have to watch them for some time to see how the already established flock reacts to the newcomers. Don't remain standing right next to the pond, however, because your presence would distract all the birds. Watch from a distance to check if the encounter is peaceful or if it is giving rise to fighting.

Fall or Winter: This is the best season for unfamiliar ducks to get to used to each other. At this time the old birds are most likely to put up with newcomers because their hormonal activity is at a low ebb (see The Reproductive Period, page 68) and the birds are consequently less aggressive. In the wild, too, many species of ducks live together peacefully during the winter.

By the time the courtship period starts in the spring, old and new ducks are so used to each other that serious conflicts are rare. On larger ponds with enough room for the birds to get away from each other if necessary, the ducks described in this book are very unlikely to fight.

Ducks that are kept in aviaries or on small garden ponds, however, see each other constantly, and this triggers aggressive behavior on the part of pairs that are ready to breed and want to defend their territory. This is one of the main reasons the number of ducks that are kept in a given yard should never be too large.

Food Intake: Be sure to check that the new birds are really eating. Sometimes the old ones don't let them near the feeding stations. Ducks can live without food for a long time. Wild mallards, for instance, can manage without food for two weeks if they are in good nutritional condition. So the fact that your ducks are still alive after one week does not mean that they have been eating regularly. To be on the safe side you should always set up several feeding stations located at some distance from each other. This arrangement should permit the newcomers to get sufficient food.

Cover: Make sure the yard offers enough cover so that ducks pursued by other aggressive birds can find hiding places to escape to and rest. The saying "out of sight, out of mind" aptly describes the behavior of birds. When optical contact with the victim ceases, pursuit is usually abandoned by the agressor.

Tameness: If your new ducks are very timid, you should always move quietly in their yard. Ducks are by nature apprehensive and always ready to take off in flight. This is true of ornamental ducks as well as utility breeds. Domestic ducks hardly ever get as tame and friendly as geese, for instance. This is one reason why farms raising ducks for market try to avoid changes in the personnel in charge of the birds and why visitors are not allowed in the duck buildings. The birds would get so excited and upset that it might interfere with their putting on weight.

Ornamental ducks don't become as friendly toward their keepers as geese do either. But in time your birds may build up sufficient confidence and trust to take food from your hand.

Care and Maintenance

Keeping Ducks in an Aviary

Aviaries are used almost exclusively for certain kinds of ornamental ducks. There is no doubt that an area that is enclosed with wire mesh on all sides offers certain advantages over an open pond.

• Small and very valuable ornamental species are protected from predators.
• The birds get all the food they are given. On a pond, wild mallards flying in from surrounding areas may compete for it.
• It is much easier to control breeding in an aviary than in an open yard with a pond. Since many species, such as the red-crested pochard, the rosy-bill, the spotbill duck, the cinnamon teal, and the blue-winged teal, commonly crossbreed when they are kept together, aviaries for housing individual pairs are essential to obtain purebred offspring.

Keeping Ducks on a Pond

Keeping ducks on a pond in an unenclosed yard has the advantage that you can watch them without the visual interference of wire mesh. By planting the surroundings of the pond imaginatively (see Planting the Pond and Its Surroundings, page 15) you can create miniature landscapes that often bear considerable resemblance to the ducks' natural habitat. The great drawback is that predators, both on the ground and from the air, have easy access to the ducks, their eggs, and the baby ducklings. Also, quite a few strangers will come as uninvited guests, leading to greater food consumption and consequently increased costs. And, as mentioned above, crossbreeding is almost inevitable if several related species are kept together (see Keeping Ducks in an Aviary, page 33). Since male hybrids never have the same brightness of plumage as normal males of the species, they cannot be sold to fanciers and therefore usually end up in the soup pot.

Diving to escape. If they sense immediate danger, all ducks quickly dive out of sight. Underwater they use their wings to swim faster; they also change direction abruptly and surface in unexpected places.

In China and some socialist republics of eastern Europe, as in East Germany, for instance, utility ducks—almost always Pekin ducks—are quite often kept and raised for market on large ponds. Raising ducks by this method is relatively cheap because the birds forage for most of their food and receive only supplementary feedings. Whether ducks can reach their optimal weight under this system is, however, questionable and obviously depends on how plentiful the food is in a particular body of water.

Keeping Ducks Indoors

Ornamental as well as utility ducks are kept indoors primarily to keep them out of the winter cold and secondarily to protect them against predators. When their pond freezes, the ducks move into their winter quarters. A number of ornamental ducks that are native to the tropics and, among utility ducks, the muscovy duck, which comes originally from South America, can easily freeze their toes and webs if they are out in the snow and ice (see page 66).

Commercial ducks are locked in their houses at night year round to keep them safe from martens, foxes, cats, and dogs; during the day they are usually let out into runs that are enclosed with fences 16 inches (40 cm) high.

Only ducks raised for market are generally kept indoors all the time to avoid a slowing of weight gain on account of too much physical activity.

Letting Ducks Roam

Utility Ducks

If you have a meadow or a field for grazing livestock, with or without a body of water, you should turn your ducks loose on it (see A Duck Pasture, page 31). There is no need to worry that your ducks might fly off because most commercial ducks are no longer capable of taking to the air. If you should have a breed that can still fly, such as muscovies, high-nesting flying ducks, or call ducks, there is still no reason for concern. If you offer them some food every evening, such as a handful of grain per bird, the birds will return punctually to their shelter to get it. Earthbound ducks like Pekins, Rouens, Aylesburies, and Indian runners will come, too, waddling as fast as their feet will carry them to the feeders to get their evening treat.

Ornamental Ducks

Letting ornamental ducks run free on unfenced land is not a good idea. Birds that have been rendered flightless wander far afield, tend to get lost, and are an easy prey for predators. With ornamental ducks you always have to remember essentially that you are dealing with wild animals that have either no bond to humans at all or at best a very tenuous one.

Some nature lovers wonder why the ponds and other bodies of water in our parks are populated primarily by swans and why some equally beautiful ornamental ducks are not to be found there. The reason is primarily practical. The ducks would have to share their food with many wild birds and would therefore have to be fed four or five times a day. The money budgeted by park administrators for feeding wildlife is rather modest in most cases and doesn't usually permit the purchase of food in the required amounts.

You should turn ducks loose in your garden or backyard only if fences keep flowerbeds and the vegetable patch out of reach of ever-hungry duck bills (see Planting the Pond and Its Surroundings, page 15). Of course the area for your ornamental ducks, which should include a pond and some dry land, has to be fenced, too, and it should take in as much grassy area as feasible. Since ducks crop the grass quite close to the ground, you can usually retire your lawnmower and replace it with this truly organic system of lawn care.

Rendering Ducks Flightless and Letting Them Fly Freely

All ornamental ducks are fast and agile flyers. Among commercial ducks only a few breeds have retained their ability to fly. Among these are the high-nesting flying duck, the call duck, the East Indie, and the muscovy duck. The other breeds, including Pekin, Aylesbury, and Rouen ducks, are much too heavy to fly or, like the Indian runner, have changed so much in body shape as a result of selective breeding that they couldn't get airborne no matter how hard they tried.

Anyone who has ducks that can fly and lets them roam freely has to be especially careful that they

Mallard ducks
Above: A tame mallard is eating out of its keeper's hand.
Below: Downy young ducklings.

don't take off for good some day. With large collections of ornamental ducks, where it is hard to keep track of all the birds because of their great number, it is not uncommon for young ducks to disappear when they have learned to fly.

Rendering Ducks Flightless: One can keep birds from flying either temporarily or permanently. In the temporary method the primaries of one wing are trimmed with scissors. The permanent method consists of pinioning, that is, removing a few small bones that support the wing on one side.

Caution: In some countries this kind of manipulation is subject to animal welfare legislation. In several European countries, for instance, only veterinarians are allowed to perform the operation, and it is permitted only when required for the animal's own welfare. You should check with your veterinarian or with appropriate authorities to find out if there are any laws of this kind in effect in your state.

When the feathers of one wing are trimmed, they will grow in again after the next molt (see page 67), and the duck will once again be able to fly. You therefore have to watch every year when the birds molt and try to catch them for wing clipping just before they regain their flying powers.

Ask someone who has done it before to show you how to trim the feathers properly.

Flying Freely: Utility breeds like the high-nesting flying duck and the muscovy are often allowed to fly as they wish on farms. These birds find most of their own food in the surrounding area and always return home in the evening to get their daily ration. However, this method is not recommended for someone living in a suburb. The unrestrained ducks would be sure to plunder all your neighbors' gardens, which would make you highly unpopular.

Various utility breeds.
Above, left: A white crested duck; above, right: A blue Indian runner.
Below: A pied blue muscovy duck.

The chicks of hole-nesting duck species have sharp little claws that enable them to climb up the steep inside walls of their nest cavities so that they can let themselves drop to the ground. Since the ducklings are light as a feather, they don't get hurt when they land on the ground below. The ducks depicted here are common goldeneyes.

Care and Maintenance

Daily Chores

When you make your morning round to check that all is as it should be in the duckyard, the first thing to do is to make sure that all the birds are still present and that none of them is sick (see page 40). Small ornamental ducks often hide in shrubbery. If they don't make an appearance when you put down food, it is a good idea to start looking for them. If females of an ornamental species suddenly disappear in the spring, this often means that they have built a nest in some hidden spot and are brooding.

After cleaning the feeders, put out only enough food to last the ducks until evening (see Feeding Ornamental Ducks, page 30). In an unenclosed yard food quickly attracts rats and mice. If the ducks have to stay indoors because of severe cold, be sure to replace their drinking and bathing water frequently. Bedding that has gotten soaked has to be either changed or covered with a layer of dry litter.

Sanitary Measures

How to Change the Pond Water

The water in your garden pond should not turn into a muddy, foul-smelling brew before you replace it with clean water. How often it needs to be changed depends on the stocking rate. Before changing the water, you should collect all the feathers, leaves, twigs, and hunks of dirt that may be floating on the water's surface—in short, anything that might plug up the drain when the pond is emptied. After removing all the debris, unscrew the overflow pipe from the drainpipe and let the water drain out.

When all the water is gone, you should shovel out the mud that has settled on the bottom. If the walls of the pond are dirty and covered with algae, they have to be scrubbed with a coarse broom or brush and regular tap water. Once all the dirt is gone, the pond walls are disinfected with a chlorine solution, which can be purchased at a garden center. Follow the directions on the package for proper dilution. After letting the chlorine work for half an hour, rinse it carefully off the walls with a garden hose. Wait until the rinse water is also completely drained out. Then screw the overflow pipe back into the drainpipe, and fill the pond with fresh water.

Follow the same procedure for cleaning a pond in an aviary. This is easier because aviary ponds are usually smaller than garden ponds.

Cleaning a Natural Pond

Small natural ponds or small craters that have filled with ground water are hard to keep clean. The most you can do is to remove dead fish and various other trash with a rake. Because these bodies of water are so hard to clean I would advise you to keep only very few ducks on such a pond in order not to disturb the biological self-cleaning action of the natural body of water. If the water starts getting dirty, the ducks should be kept away (see Botulism, page 43). Larger ponds with reed and rush growth along the edges are usually self-cleaning.

Cleaning a Duck House

Duck houses, where birds destined for market are housed crowded together, get dirty very quickly. That is why sanitation is especially important here. Whenever the litter gets wet, it has to be removed or covered with layers of dry straw. Simply covering up the soaked litter is a perfectly sanitary way of dealing with it. It is the customary method as long as the flock is healthy. In the runs of ornamental or utility ducks, droppings that have been walked on and mashed into the ground are dug up with a spade and replaced with fresh earth. Feeders and water dishes should be scrubbed daily with a coarse brush.

Whitewash: Whitewashing the walls of the duck house once a year is part of keeping the place hygienic. The lime in the whitewash solution only has minimal disinfecting power, but the solution can be made more potent by adding 4 ounces of

Lysol per gallon (118 ml per 3.78 L) or 6 ounces of Clorox per gallon (177 ml per 3.78 L). To make an effective whitewash you can mix 10 quarts (10 L) of regular whitewash with ¼ pound (125 gm) potato starch, a handful of cooking salt, and 10 ounces (295 ml) of Lysol. Whitewash solutions should be applied immediately after mixing.

Chloride of lime is not a suitable disinfectant because it has a strong chlorine smell and corrodes clothes and shoes as well as metals.

Cleaning an Aviary

In an aviary all the droppings on the ground have to be collected and removed, and the water basin, which is usually small, has to be cleaned. These are daily chores. When the breeding season is over, the nest boxes and other nest sites are taken out. Any nesting materials are discarded. The inside walls of the nest boxes are disinfected with a chlorine solution (see page 38). The boxes are then stacked and put away until the next breeding season.

Health Care and Diseases

Preventive Care

If ornamental or commercial ducks are cared for and maintained properly, they are—compared to other bird families—subject to relatively few diseases. Preventive care is of special importance, however, and it is essential that you observe the following basic rules.

- Because many infections are transmitted by way of excreta, it is important always to keep the shelters, yards, and swimming water clean (see Daily Chores and Sanitary Measures, page 38).
- Giving the ducks a good, nutritious diet even during the winter months makes them more resistant to disease and helps prevent metabolic and deficiency diseases (see Feeding, page 27).
- Newly acquired ducks must be kept separate from the established birds for at least 2 weeks because they might otherwise introduce pathogens into your flock (see Quarantine, page 32).
- New ducks have to be given time to adjust to their new situation so that they can defend themselves adequately against the established birds (see Proper Acclimation, page 32).

If a Duck Gets Sick

If you watch your birds regularly, changes in their behavior will become obvious to you very quickly (see table, page 41). A duck is sick if:

- it lies on the ground for unusually long periods of time and is reluctant to enter the water;
- its breast and abdominal feathers lack luster and look stringy;
- its natural escape reactions are slow or lacking altogether;
- it has very little or no interest in food;
- the breastbone protrudes sharply, which you can check on by feeling the breast area with your hand;
- a drake fails to grow his usual nuptial plumage in the fall.

Externally Visible Problems

Lameness

Cause: Lameness is quite common in ducks. If the birds are kept on a hard floor, whether it be tiles or packed dirt, their sensitive toes and webs suffer. The soles and the balls of the feet are compacted, which sooner or later leads to calluses. In many cases pus forms underneath the callous layer of the skin and gradually hardens into a cheeselike mass.
Symptoms: To try to minimize the pain in their feet, the ducks often lie around on land and limp into the water when people approach.
Treatment: Treating this kind of condition is difficult and a cure is far from assured. Take the affected duck to the veterinarian, who will remove the calluses and scrape out as much of the pus as possible. The foot is then bandaged, and the patient should be placed on a soft surface, such as sawdust, peat moss, or rubber mats.
Prevention: Try not to have large, hard areas in the duckyard. Concrete floors can be covered with sand, for instance, and packed dirt should frequently be spaded and hoed.

Slipped Wing

Cause: This condition is the result of weak tendons in young birds, but it is not hereditary. In utility ducks raised for market slipped wings are no serious matter, but in breeding stock and in ornamental ducks a slipped wing is a real flaw. Young muscovy ducks are especially prone to this condition.
Symptoms: The distal joints of the wings with the heavy quills within which the primaries are developing get very heavy in the growing birds and are sometimes so weighty that they twist outward and downward. As a consequence one or both wings stick out from the body at almost a right angle.
Treatment: In its early stage this condition can be cured. The veterinarian places the wing in its normal position, inserts a wad of cotton between the body and the wing, and tapes everything in place with an adhesive bandage. In addition a cotton or

Health Care and Diseases

Important Signs of Sickness

Signs	Possible Causes
Drab-looking, dry plumage	Improper diet or environmental conditions; in artificially brooded chicks, stress and insufficient secretion from the oil gland
Wing hanging down almost vertically in young ducks	slipped wing
Feather eating and feather plucking in young ducks	Boredom, particularly in market ducks raised in overcrowded conditions
Incomplete molting of drakes from eclipse to nuptial plumage	Internal disease, metabolic problem, sign of old age
Bare places on back of the head and on neck in females	Fights with other ducks, the drake grabbing her by the head feathers in the course of mating
Withering and loss of toes and webs in tropical ducks	Freezing in ice-cold water if kept on pond during winter
If the following signs are observed, it is essential to consult a veterinarian	
Pumping breathing with open bill	Aspergillosis or, possibly, salmonellosis
Retching motions of neck and head and rapid weight loss in ducklings three or more weeks old	Infestation with gizzard worms
Lying on the ground with outstretched neck and signs of paralysis	Botulism poisoning
Loss of balance, reeling	First signs of botulism poisoning, salmonellosis, or viral hepatitis
Listlessness, falling over and lying on the side, convulsive paddling motions of the feet—in ducklings two to three weeks old	Viral hepatitis
Apathy and ruffled feathers in females, often "penguin stance," sticky plumage in caudal region	Egg Binding
Plumage in caudal region smeared with runny droppings of various colors	Enteritis as a result of improper diet, poisoning, or salmonellosis
Limping	Cornlike calluses and sores on the bottom of the pads and joints of the feet; also seen with salmonellosis

linen bandage is wrapped around the body, passing both in front of and in back of the legs and across the back. After two weeks the bandages can be removed, and the wing will stay in its normal position.

Slipped wings occur in young ducks, especially in young muscovies. They are caused by weak tendons that are overtaxed by the heavy quills on the outer wing segment. When this condition occurs, one or both wings stick out from the body almost at a right angle.

Feather-Plucking and Feather-Eating

Causes: There seem to be several reasons for this pernicious habit, but it is not entirely clear what roles they all play. Feather-plucking and feather-eating are common in mass operations where many ducks are confined in small areas. The problem is especially prevalent in immature ducks at the time they lose their down and the adult plumage grows in (see The Molt, page 67).
Visible Signs: Usually the drakes that are most advanced in development start plucking the blood-filled quills of other ducklings and eating them greedily. First they bite off the feathers on their fellows' backs, then they move on to the wings and to other parts of the body.
Treatment: A number of methods to try to stop feather-eating have been tried, such as increasing the protein content in the ducks' diet and changing the lighting in the duck houses—without significant results so far.

Dry Plumage

Cause: The problem is that the down plumage of baby ducklings that were hatched by a broody hen or in an artificial incubator was insufficiently oiled or not oiled at all. When ducklings are brooded by their mother, their downy plumage becomes water-repellent through contact with the parent bird's plumage. Ducklings are born with the innate ability to grease their feathers with the secretions of their oil glands, but during the first few days the glands are not productive enough to waterproof the plumage adequately.
Visible signs: Ducklings incubated by broody hens or in artificial incubators drown when they try to swim because their dry feathers get waterlogged.
Treatment: If you should witness such an incident, quickly grab the duckling from the water, rub its feathers dry, and set it under a heat lamp.
Prevention: Keep all baby ducklings—both ornamental and utility breeds—that were not brooded by ducks away from water at first. Then introduce them to water gradually by setting up shallow basins. Their uropygial glands will soon start secreting oil so that the ducklings can grease their feathers themselves. Many breeders of ornamental and commercial ducks who want to avoid all risk don't let their ducklings near water until the down on their breasts and abdomens has been replaced by permanent feathers.

Internal Diseases

Salmonellosis

Cause: Bacteria of the genus *Salmonella* are the causative agents of this disease, which can spread like an epidemic and cause huge losses where ducks are raised on a large scale. The immediate cause of an outbreak may be dirty eggshells, insufficiently disinfected incubators or rearing boxes, or generally unsanitary conditions in the brooder house. Among laying ducks there are quite often some that constantly eliminate salmonella bacteria in their excreta. Or the droppings of a single sick duckling may spread the disease throughout the entire flock in no time at all. Since ornamental ducks are hardly ever kept or raised in large numbers, the disease is rare among them. Salmonellosis is transmissible to humans. If there are small children in your household, you should not let them get near the droppings of the birds.

Symptoms: Ducks suffering from salmonellosis often show no clear symptoms. The most common signs are diarrhea, lameness caused by swollen joints, and paralysis. Sick ducklings often sit in groups under the heat lamp with raised feathers and half-closed eyes. Death may follow quickly or not until after several days of sickness. Birds that survive the sickness harbor the dangerous bacteria and pass them on in their droppings and their eggs for the rest of their lives.

A sick duck is reluctant to swim. It will lie on the ground for long periods of time with closed eyes, its plumage in disarray, and produce frequent, runny droppings.

Treatment: An absolutely foolproof diagnosis of salmonellosis is possible only through a bacteriological analysis of the droppings or the organs of deceased birds. That is why, if you suspect the disease, you should send droppings and cadavers to a veterinary laboratory as quickly as possible. Sick ducklings can be cured with antibiotics, but the high cost and the need for prolonged treatment make it uneconomical to try to save the birds.

Botulism (Limberneck)

Cause: In the late summer and early fall, mass dying is sometimes caused by the bacterium *Clostridium botulinum* among ducks and other waterfowl on park waters. The disease tends to occur in bodies of water without outlets and in still bays of lakes during dry summers with lots of sunshine. In the warm oxygen-deficient water botulism bacteria multiply rapidly in mud and decaying animal matter. The ducks get sick from ingesting decaying vegetable and animal matter and maggots containing the toxin produced by the bacteria, a toxin that is one of the most deadly organic nerve poisons in existence. According to current medical opinion there is no danger of the poisoning spreading to humans that touch sick or dead ducks, their droppings, or the contaminated water and mud in a duck pond.

Symptoms: Depending on the amount and concentration of the toxin absorbed, the ducks may die within a few hours without any previous signs of illness or lie on the shore, paralyzed but conscious, with half-closed eyes and straight necks because they have lost control over their neck muscles.

Treatment: There is no promising treatment. Birds that have absorbed only minimal amounts of poison sometimes recover.

Prevention: Keep healthy ducks away from contaminated waters. In a sisml natural pond you can search the bottom with nets for dead animals and pipe fresh water into the pond. This deprives the botulism bacteria of the medium in which they thrive. There is no botulism vaccine for ducks.

Infectious Hepatitis (Virus Hepatitis)

Cause: This form of hepatitis is caused by a virus and accounts for great losses among ducklings two to three weeks old. The virus is ingested in food and droppings, and it is also absorbed from the air. It is not communicable to humans.

Symptoms: Affected ducklings suffer from disturbed equilibrium, lie on their sides, have their heads drawn back toward their tails, and make

convulsive paddling motions with their legs. The sickness often lasts no more than one day and generally ends in death. When the dead body is cut open, the liver is conspicuously enlarged, yellow, and full of dot-like hemorrhages.
Treatment: If there is an outbreak of viral hepatitis in a flock, vaccination can save the ducklings that are still healthy. In such flocks vaccinating the breeding ducks two weeks to a month before egg laying is recommended because the mother's immunity is passed through the egg to the offspring.

Aspergillosis (Brooder Pneumonia)

Cause: The causative agent, a fungus of the *Aspergillus* genus, is found worldwide and especially affects very young ducklings but sometimes mature ducks as well. The fungus forms a grayish-green to blackish mold on damp feed, dirty litter, and decaying organic material of all kinds. The spores become airborne at the slightest air movement and are then inhaled by the ducks. In healthy birds the spores remain inactive; but in ducks whose resistance is lowered as a result of improper environmental conditions, colds, or the strain of lengthy transport, they propagate; a solid lining of fungi forms on the moist inside walls of the respiratory organs, leading to clogging of narrow passages, such as the bronchia. The fungi also produce highly toxic waste substances that affect the bird's entire organism.
Symptoms: Affected birds gasp for breath while opening and shutting their bills rhythmically. Eventually they suffocate.
Treatment and Prevention: Aspergillosis is not transmitted from a sick animal to healthy ones. There is at this point no effective medication against the fungus, although various drugs on the market claim to alleviate the disease.

The best precaution to take against the disease is to disinfect the housing and the incubating rooms regularly. The incubators, too, have to be disinfected both before the eggs are placed in them and after the ducklings hatch. Damp litter, droppings, and all spilled food should always be removed just as promptly as possible (see Sanitary Measures, page 38).

Gizzard Worms

Cause: The *Echinuria* worm is transmitted to ducks by way of water fleas. These tiny crustaceans ingest the worm eggs in their food, and the eggs develop into larvae within a few days. If water fleas with worm larvae find their way into a duck's stomach, the parasites burrow deep into the lining of the stomach where they form cysts the size of a lentil or a pea that protrude bulblike, often densely covering an area. These protruberances can block the narrow passage between the proventriculus and the gizzard and thus keep the food from moving on. The blockage in the proventriculus distends the stomach walls and weakens the stomach muscles.
Symptoms: Ducklings three to eight weeks of age are most likely to become infested. They become listless and lose interest in eating. At the same time they often make retching motions while shaking their heads violently. After a few days they succumb to weakness. Treatment: When worms have been positively identified as the cause of death of one or more young ducklings, the rest of the flock can be saved through immediate treatment by the veterinarian with Piperazine or Levamisol. Ducklings that survive an infestation harbor only a few of the parasites but keep eliminating worm eggs in their droppings.

The most effective hygienic measure to prevent worm infestation is to keep the ducklings off bodies of water where the worms are established and let them swim instead on artificial ponds without water fleas. Once the ducks are fully grown the worms no longer present a danger.

Egg-Binding

Cause: There are a number of reasons why a duck may be unable to pass an egg out of the oviduct. The egg may be abnormally large or misshapen, or have too soft a shell. The condition often occurs in ducks laying their first eggs or ones that have been overly productive in the past; it can also be the result of environmental factors like a rapid and dramatic change in temperature. Eggs that lack the hard shell covering the egg skin adapt elastically to the wave-like contractions of the oviduct muscles without moving downward. Big eggs get stuck because of their size.

Symptoms: A duck in this predicament often sits on the ground very straight in "penguin position," ruffles its feathers, and keeps its eyes shut. The lower abdomen protrudes balloonlike and feels hot to the touch, and the caudal feathers may be dirty with a sticky discharge, feces, and sand.

Treatment: The best thing to do is to take the duck to the veterinarian. If that is impossible, insert a syringe (without the needle!) filled with warm oil (salad oil or paraffin oil) into the opening of the oviduct, and slowly empty the syringe. If you can feel the egg from the outside, you can try to move it toward the cloaca by massaging the area very gently. But breaking an egg that is stuck by applying too much pressure from the outside is dangerous for the bird. The sharp shell fragments can injure the delicate mucous lining of the oviduct.

What Can You Do to Help a Sick Duck?

Isolate sick ducks from the rest of the flock. This is done to prevent the sickness from spreading to the other ducks and to provide quiet for the sick one.

Plan ahead and make sure you have an "infirmary" ready. There the bird is placed on something soft, like a rubber mat, and given a shallow dish with food and one with water within bill's reach. If the patient refuses to eat, it may have to be force-fed.

The Visit to the Veterinarian

If the bird has something external wrong, like a skin injury, or if you suspect broken bones, you should take it to the veterinarian. The same applies to internal diseases because most of them have only fairly general, unspecific symptoms. Call the veterinarian first and set up an appointment. The duck is then caught and put into a large shopping bag with handles or into a basket with a cover that can be hooked or tied shut. A shopping bag should be lined with cloth. Place a light cloth over the top that will not cut off air for breathing. The semidark also has a calming influence on the duck.

If one of your ducks dies, the body should not be disposed of but sent as quickly as possible to a veterinary laboratory to establish the cause of death. These post-mortems are not free of charge, but if the bird died of some contagious disease, you can then treat and save the rest of the flock, and the cost of the autopsy was well worth while. If an infectious disease was diagnosed, you should call your veterinarian to have him treat your flock and advise you on how to prevent the disease in the future.

Raising Ducks

Necessary Conditions

There are some very basic differences between raising utility ducks and raising ornamental ducks. The former is a commercial enterprise of growing economic importance, while the latter activity is confined almost exclusively to duck fanciers.

Utility Ducks

Today utility ducks are raised primarily to be sold as roast ducklings. On a much smaller scale, ducks are raised for breeding stock to maintain and improve individual breeds. The production of eggs for human consumption and of down is insignificant compared to the meat industry.

For duck raising to be economically productive you must follow certain rules that you should be aware of.

• Use only fully grown stock for breeding. Heavyweight breeds like Rouen and Aylesbury ducks reach sexual maturity at one year of age; Pekin ducks and other medium-heavy to light breeds are fully mature at six months.
• First establish your breeding groups. A breeding group consists of a drake and several females. (One drake and two ducks are called a trio; a drake with four or five ducks are a pen.) The highest fertility rates are achieved in light breeds with four or five ducks per drake and in heavy breeds with a two or three ducks per drake. It is best to combine the birds in the fall for them to get used to each other.

Flying chases like this are often seen in the spring. A strange drake is pursuing a bonded female, trying to grab her by the tail, and the female's mate is chasing the interloper with similar intentions.

• Since heavy breeds achieve better fertility rates if they mate in the water, they should have at least a small swim basin in their enclosure.
• Birds selected for breeding should conform to their breed standard, that is, they should have all the qualities that the standard for that particular breed calls for. This includes not only coloration of the plumage but also meat quality, egg production, and weight.

As a *general rule* you can assume that breeding ducks of both sexes is still productive in their fifth year. Females start laying at about 140 to 180 days of age. Good breeder ducks should be lively birds that are continually active in the search for food. If their plumage is still smooth and hugs the body closely at the end of the laying period, this indicates a good layer.

On the other hand, if the feathers remain wet a long time after bathing, this is a sign of poor constitution. It is assumed by breeders that the constitution of the parent birds is reflected in the quality of the offspring. This does not necessarily mean, however, that the ducklings of good parent birds are always strong and hardy, especially if the parent birds have not been adequately fed (see Feeding Laying Ducks, page 29) and were kept in runs that were too small for them. If the breeder birds are not given proper care, the proportion of fertile eggs declines, embryos die inside the eggs, and the ducklings that do hatch are weak. It is worth remembering this before poor hatching results are blamed exclusively on faulty incubators.

Ornamental Ducks

Ornamental ducks are essentially wild ducks and are, in contrast to domestic ducks, monogamous. That is why ornamental ducks are always combined in pairs. Since each pair establishes its own territory during the courtship and laying period and defends this territory against other pairs, fights may break out in small enclosures. Although most of these conflicts do not end in fatalities, they are upsetting to the birds and can interfere with breeding so that no offspring are produced. On a larger body of water where potential antagonists have a chance to avoid each other, such problems are less frequent. But breeding success is most likely if only one pair of ducks is kept in an aviary (see page 33).

What About Protected Species?

In 1973 an agreement, called The Convention on International Trade in Endangered Species of Wild Fauna and Flora (CITES), was drawn up in Washington, D.C. It regulates international trade in wild animals and plants and lists endangered species, grouped in three appendices reflecting how serious the threat of extinction is. Individual classifications are not permanent but can be changed at any time to reflect more current information.

The species covered by the Convention are grouped into three categories.

Appendix I: Species threatened with extinction which are or may be affected by trade.

Appendix II: Comprises species which although not necessarily now threatened with extinction, may become so unless trade is strictly regulated to avoid utilization incompatible with their survival. Also included in this appendix are species which are listed because of their visual similarity to other Appendix I and II species.

Appendix III: Contains species which any party identifies as being subject to regulation within its own jurisdiction for the purpose of preventing or restricting exploitation, and as needing the cooperation of other parties in the control of trade.

In addition to live specimens, the Convention also applies to eggs, feathers and any other parts and derivatives which can be identified as belonging to a listed species. In some instances species are listed on CITES only with respect to certain subspecies or geographically separate populations. Imports or exports of Appendix I specimens are authorized only in exceptional circumstances. These exceptional circumstances under which licenses *may* be granted fall into four main categories.

• Personal or household effects.
• Captive-bred specimens.
• Noncommercial loans, donations, or exchanges between registered scientists or institutions.
• Traveling zoos or circuses.

Imports of Appendix I and II specimens are generally permitted provided that the appropriate export documentation is presented.

For more information contact:
Chief of the Federal Wildlife Permit Office,
Room 611, Broyhill Building,
1000 North Glebe Road,
Arlington, VA 22201

Nest Sites

Wild Ducks

In their natural habitat wild ducks lay their eggs hidden in bushes, large tufts of grass, stands of reeds, or other vegetation. Wood ducks and mandarin ducks always nest above the ground in tree holes. Only the uniquely adaptable mallard will make its nest just about anywhere.

If you keep ornamental or wild ducks in aviaries or on ponds, you have to make sure they have artificial nest sites (see Keeping Ducks in an Aviary, Keeping Ducks on a Pond, page 33). If there are enough plants to provide cover, you can dig shallow hollows in the earth between them and cover the hollows with hay, straw, or dry leaves. Ducks often accept small doghouses, horizontally placed barrels, fruit crates, or a small A-frame made of a few boards—all kinds of shelters into which the birds can retreat—and use them for nesting.

Hole nesters, like the wood duck and the mandarin duck, insist even in captivity on nest boxes or cavities that are at least 20 inches (50 cm) off the ground. These can be mounted on posts. You can provide access for birds whose wings are clipped by leaning a small wooden ladder or a split log against the box just below the entry hole.

Nest sites. Wild or ornamental ducks like to nest hidden in boxes that look like houses or under reed roofs. Hole nesters prefer cavities that are at least 20 inches (50 cm) above ground.

1. Nest cavity for ground-breeding species and tree-breeding species that are allowed to fly.
2. A nest house for ducks.
3. A nest house with a chicken ladder for tree-nesting species.
4. A duck nest protected by an A-frame made of two boards.
5. A simple reed hut.
6. A duck nest with a reed roof and a chicken ladder leading into the water.

Domestic Ducks

Of the many domestic duck breeds only a few—namely, ducks that still resemble their ancestor, the mallard duck, brood their own eggs. Among these breeds are the high-nesting flying duck, the call duck, and the East Indie duck. Completely unrelated to these is the muscovy duck, which also still broods its own eggs. Set up nests in the duck house for these broody ducks.

Since muscovies are hole nesters, their nests should be off the ground and reachable by way of a chicken ladder. High-nesting flying ducks accept nests on the ground as well as raised ones. Both the East Indie and the call duck nest on the ground. The best location for the nests is along the side and back walls of the building. There the ducks brood happily in flat crates that are filled with straw or hay.

The females of highly developed domestic breeds, on the other hand, have lost their brooding instinct almost entirely and simply drop their eggs wherever they happen to be. Some of them occasionally do lay eggs in a nest, but they are unreliable brooders or abandon the eggs altogether. You have to collect the eggs you find lying on the ground every day.

Natural Incubation

Natural incubation means that the eggs are brooded by the duck that laid them or by a foster mother that can be a duck or a chicken.

Wild ducks are usually steady brooders unless they are disturbed by having to share their living space with too many other birds. It stands to reason that successful natural brooding and crowding of the duck enclosures are mutually exclusive. In unprotected areas, on the other hand, the baby ducklings are exposed to many dangers because crows, magpies, martens, cats, and other predators all take their toll. That is why it is better not to let the natural mother brood her clutch and lead her young about in unprotected surroundings. Instead, put the eggs under a reliable foster mother, whether duck or chicken. Or you can brood the eggs artificially with the aid of an electric incubator (see Artificial Incubation, page 51).

Collecting the Eggs

If you decide not to let your female ornamental ducks sit on their eggs, you have to remove the eggs from the nests every day. But always leave a chicken egg or a fake egg in the nest. This way the laying ornamental female will not get discouraged but will go on laying in the same nest. Because ducks keep laying longer when a full clutch fails to accumulate, you will end up with many more eggs than you would if you let the natural mother sit on the clutch.

Marking the Eggs

Eggs, from both ornamental and domestic ducks, that are to be incubated either by a foster mother or in an artificial incubator should have the name of the breed or species and the laying date marked on the shell. This allows you to keep track of each egg and the productiveness of the ducks. It also makes it possible for you to make up clutches combining eggs of the same species or breed. In the case of ornamental ducks this is important because the eggs of many wild species are so similar that it would be impossible to tell them apart without the data written on them. On commercial duck farms, where generally only one breed is raised, the date of laying is all that has to be noted.

Washing the Eggs

The eggs of domestic ducks are often smeared with wet droppings, which have to be carefully washed off. The droppings may harbor pathogens that could develop and multiply in the humid, warm environment of the incubator and later lead to massive losses among the hatched ducklings (see Salmonellosis, page 42).

Dirty eggs should be placed for a few minutes in a 0.1% potassium permanganate solution, which softens the caked dirt and kills many of the germs in it. Afterward the eggs are carefully wiped off with a soft sponge.

Large duck-raising establishments routinely fumigate all eggs with formalin before placing them in the incubator.

Storing the Eggs

Eggs collected from ornamental and commercial ducks are stored in a special room before they are incubated. This is necessary first of all because you have to accumulate enough eggs to form a clutch before you can give them to a broody bird or place them in an incubator. More important, the tiny embryos inside the eggs start developing slowly even below the optimal brooding temperature of 100°F (37.8°C), and incorrect storage temperatures and air conditions can lead to premature death of embryos.

The room where the eggs are stored should be 59° to 65°F (15°–18°C) and have a humidity level of 70%. Especially during the warm part of the year it is true that the shorter the waiting period before incubation, the greater the proportion of the eggs that hatch. Duck eggs lose their viability more quickly than do chicken eggs and should ideally not be stored longer than a week before incubation. During the waiting period the eggs should be turned at least three times a day. Before the eggs are given to a foster mother or put in an incubator, they should be kept for several hours in a warmer room because a sudden change from a rather cool to a warm environment can prove fatal to the embryo.

Ducks as Foster Mothers

Probably the most ideal foster mother for brooding the eggs of ornamental as well as utility ducks is the muscovy. Muscovies get broody three times a year, are reliable brooders, and also mother the baby ducklings well. It is a good idea to have several muscovy ducks so that at least one of them is likely to be broody when need arises. Call ducks have also proven good foster mothers, especially for clutches of small ornamental ducks.

Eggs of utility ducks that have lost their brooding instinct can also be given to muscovies to raise.

The muscovy duck is a very popular utility duck and is especially good for sitting on eggs from ornamental or utility ducks. The wild muscovy (above) comes from South America and is smaller and lighter than the big domesticated strain (below; see also photo on page 37).

Large operations, however, where tens of thousands of ducklings are raised for market, obviously prefer artificial incubation for practical reasons.

A duck that serves as foster mother has to lay her own eggs before she is ready to sit. In the case of muscovies, a clutch will consist of about 15 eggs. When the clutch is complete, you can replace it with the eggs of another species. A muscovy duck can sit on 15 or at most 20 eggs. The rule of thumb that applies to all ducks brooding eggs other than their own is that no more should be given to them than they can cover with their bodies.

Chickens as Foster Mothers

It is common practice today to take duck eggs away from broody chickens shortly before hatching time and place them in a hatching incubator. Depending on the size of the eggs and the breed or species of duck, a broody chicken can cover a clutch of 8 to 10 duck eggs. The eggs have to be moistened regularly with a plant mister because the plumage of a chicken is drier than that of a duck. You can do the spraying when the chicken leaves the nest to eat and drink. Since a chicken is unable to grease the baby ducklings with oil from her uropygial gland (see Dry Plumage, page 42), the baby ducklings must be kept away from swimming water for the first few days.

It sometimes happens that chickens serving as foster mothers to ducklings kill the latter when they hatch because the voices of the baby birds sound unfamiliar to them. Since it tends to be the same chickens that keep killing baby ducklings, these birds should be eliminated as foster mothers. But there is another way to use these "baby murderers." Take the duck eggs away from the brooding hen shortly before hatching and place them in an incubator where they can hatch safely.

Occasionally, broody chickens leave a clutch of duck eggs prematurely because chicken eggs take only 21 days to hatch, whereas duck eggs require 21 to 35 days of incubation, depending on the species. In this case, too, the eggs should be placed in an incubator at the end until the ducklings hatch.

Turning the eggs. A duck mother turns her eggs every few hours during incubation. This is crucial for the normal development of the embryos, which would die if left in the same position.

Artificial Incubation

Duck eggs can be artificially brooded in incubators that are generally heated by electricity. There are two basic types: still-air and forced-air incubators. The first type is designed for one layer of eggs, while in the second, several trays of eggs are stacked on top of each other.

Sometimes people also speak of starter incubators and hatching incubators. Both can be of either of the two types mentioned above, and they differ from each other only in function. Eggs are placed in a starter incubator at the beginning of incubation and left there until shortly before they are due to hatch. Then they are placed in a hatching incubator, where the ducklings actually emerge from their shells. This method of using two incubators has proven advantageous for practical and hygienic reasons.

Candling Eggs

Eggs can be candled in a darkened room with a commercially available egg candler. Candling is done to see if eggs are fertile and later to find out in good time if an embryo has died and the egg is beginning to rot. Duck eggs should be candled on the 7th, 14th, and 22nd day of incubation.

• Infertile eggs show up clear with the yolk appearing only faintly. The air space cell has increased in size.
• Fertile eggs show a small, dark spot with tiny blood vessels branching out from it. From the 14th day on they are opaque and appear almost black.
• An embryo that has started to develop and then died appears as a dark, floating blot that is sometimes stuck to the inside of the shell.

Incubation Factors

The 6 most important factors affecting incubation are temperature, air, humidity, rotation, turning, and cooling.

Temperature probably has the most crucial effect on the development of the chick inside the egg. In an artificial incubator it can be precisely regulated by means of a thermostat. The table below shows the exact incubation temperatures necessary for duck eggs.

Air flow carries heat, humidity, and fresh air to the different parts of the incubator. To achieve as even an air circulation as possible, forced-air incubators are equipped with vents and fans. There are incubators with rapid and with slower air circulation. For incubating duck eggs, slower air circulation seems to work better. Set the fan in such a way that the air is renewed in the incubator 8 to 10 times per hour. Duck embryos have a higher metabolism rate than chicken embryos. The temperature and the relative air humidity should be set as follows for eggs of domestic ducks and mallards:

Day	Temperature	Relative humidity (%)	Incubator
1–24	99.7°–100.0°F (37.6°–37.8°C)	50–70	Starter
25–28	99.1°–99.5°F (37.3°–37.5°C)	70–90	Hatching

Humidity inside the incubator is regulated by a contact thermometer that is connected to a humidifier. If your incubator is not equipped with this kind of automatic system, you should moisten the eggs once a day with a plant mister filled with lukewarm water. Increased humidity toward the end of incubation is very important if waterfowl eggs are artificially incubated. That is why the relative air humidity is set higher in the hatching incubator than in the starting incubator.

Rotating refers to the way a mother duck keeps moving the eggs around with her bill. Thus the eggs that were on the outside of the clutch are gradually moved to the center and vice versa, with the result that the brooding warmth is shared equally. In an attempt to imitate this system, the breeder should move the eggs around in the incubator every day and turn them at the same time.

Turning of the eggs is crucial for the normal development of the embryos. A mother duck turns her eggs every couple of hours which, during an incubation period of 26 days, adds up to some 500 turnings. She turns them 90°, 180°, and 360°. If the eggs were not turned, the embryos would get stuck to the yolks and to the egg membranes and would perish.

Eggs that are artificially incubated need to be turned several times a day, too. There are modern incubators with timers and electric motors that automatically tilt the egg trays every hour or two first 90° to one side, then 90° to the other. If your incubator lacks these technical refinements, you will have to turn the eggs manually a minimum of 3 times a day and always by 180°. To keep track of which eggs have been turned and which have not, it is helpful to mark each egg with different symbols on opposite sides, for instance, 1 and 2, or M and E. By starting out with the same symbol on the top of every egg, you can see at a glance if you have neglected to turn one. Four days before the hatching date the eggs should no longer be turned, and they should be moved from the starter to the hatching incubator.

Cooling the incubating eggs is also important. In nature, the brooding duck leaves her clutch once a day for a half hour to eat and defecate, and the eggs may cool down by 14° to 18°F (8°–10°C). This brief daily drop in temperature not only has no harmful effect on the embryos but, on the contrary, improves their vigor because it allows for an increased ex-

Scenes from duck life.
Above, left: White muscovy duck flapping its wings; above, right: upending mallard female. Below: A pair of red-crested pochards during the courtship period.

change of gases through the porous eggshell. More oxygen enters through the pores in the egg membrane and into the vascular system of the embryo, and more carbonic acid is dissipated by the same route.

In artificial incubation we attempt to duplicate this process. From the 10th day until the chicks start pipping, the eggs are periodically allowed to cool. This is done by opening the incubator two or three times a day for 15 to 20 minutes, leaving the fans running, to let the eggs cool down to 86°F (30°C). The cooling should always be done before the eggs are moved around and turned. Experiments comparing eggs that are cooled and eggs that are not cooled during artificial incubation have clearly shown that the first method produces superior hatching results.

Proper position of the egg at hatching time is also crucial for normal births. The blunt end with the air chamber should be raised slightly but no more than 45°. This is the easiest position for the chick to break through the cell membrane so that it can breathe in the oxygen. If the pointed end were raised, the chick would try to turn its head up but would be unable to do so and would suffocate for lack of air.

Incubation Periods for Different Kinds of Ducks

Since the incubation period for ducks varies from 21 to 35 days, it is important to know how long the eggs of your ducks will take to hatch. The following list gives the different lengths.

Mallards and domestic ducks descended from them:	26–29 days
Spotbill Duck	26–28 days
Pintail	21–23 days
Gadwall	25–27 days
Falcated Teal	25–26 days
Northern Shoveler	25–27 days
European Wigeon	22–25 days
American Wigeon	22–25 days
Chiloe Wigeon	24–25 days
Green-winged Teal	21–23 days
Garganey	21–25 days
Cinnamon Teal	24–25 days
Blue-winged Teal	24–26 days
Baikal Teal	23– 26 days
Bahama Pintail	25–26 days
Silver Teal	24– 26 days
Ringed Teal	23 days
Mandarin Duck	31 days
Wood Duck	8–32 days
Muscovy Duck	35 days
Red-crested Pochard	26–28 days
Rosy-bill	27–29 days
European Pochard	24–26 days
Tufted Duck	23–25 days
Ferruginous Duck	25–27 days
Ruddy Duck	23– 26 days
Common Goldeneye	27–32 days

Hatching Ducklings

Depending on the species, a duckling breaks through the inner membrane that separates it from the air cell sometime between the 21st and the 35th day of incubation. The egg tooth, a small, hard bump on the tip of the upper mandible, is used to puncture the membrane. Now the chick has enough air to breathe; the air cell or air chamber at this point takes up a fourth of the space inside the shell, having increased as moisture evaporated.

Vocal Contact: Ducklings begin to breathe and

Different utility breeds.
Above, left: A white American Pekin duck; above, right: Rouen duck; center, left: Orpington duck; center, right: Altrhein magpie duck; Below, left: Cayuga duck; below, right: High-nesting flying ducks, pied wild color.

chirp three days before they actually hatch. If they are naturally brooded, the mother duck responds to their chirps with soft sounds of her own and thus establishes vocal contact with her offspring very early. In an incubator the ducklings have to make do without their mother's voice, but this lack has no negative effect on the hatching process or the ducklings' later development.

Breaking Out of the Shell: When the duckling is ready to emerge from the shell, it presses its bill with the egg tooth against the inside wall on the blunt end of the egg and bores a small hole through it. This is called pipping. Once the initial hole is made, the chick continues pipping and at the same time slowly rotates inside the shell by pushing with its left leg until a ring-shaped crack develops and the top of the shell is ready to lift off. Kicking with both feet, the duckling eventually makes its way out of the shell and then just lies there for a while, exhausted from the effort. The damp down that clings to its body dries off within half an hour to an hour in the incubator or under the mother duck's wings, and then the baby duckling appears the way we all picture ducklings, cute and fluffy. The hatching process from the beginning of pipping until the duckling leaves the egg takes about 12 hours.

Artificial Rearing

Wild Baby Ducklings: Newly hatched wild ducklings hide timidly when the incubator door is first opened. If you try to get hold of one, it may jump out in a flash and quickly scuttle across the floor to a dark corner, where it hunkers down motionless. This is an indication that the predator image, or the panic response at the approach of a large creature, is inborn. Later on, the ducklings will get used to their caretaker and even take food from his or her hand; however, they don't like to be touched and don't follow that person around. Wild baby ducklings that have lost their mother when several days old are hard to rear because of their

The Hatching process

a. Depending on the species, duck eggs are incubated from 21 to 35 days.

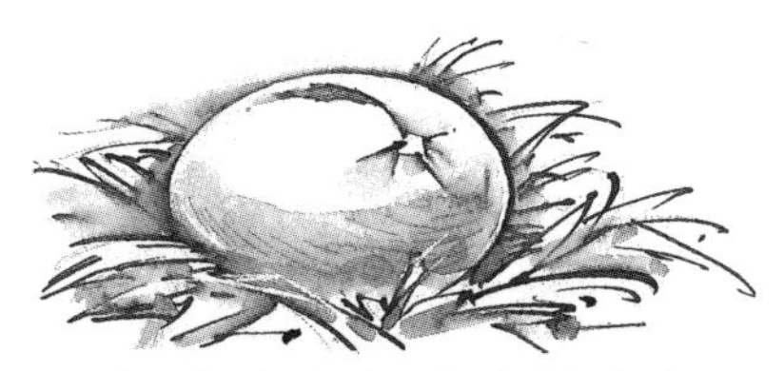

b. Here the duckling is pipping the shell by boring a small hole in it with its egg tooth.

c. Now the duckling is struggling its way out of the shell.

d. Exhausted from the effort of hatching, the baby duckling just lies there for a while.

great fear of human beings. They keep trying to escape, are extremely shy, and accept food only reluctantly. The chances of helping them survive are therefore slim.

Domestic Ducks: Our domestic varieties have largely lost this instinctive fear of humans in the course of domestication.

The Brooder Box: Whether you are dealing with wild or domestic ducklings, you will have to move them from the incubator into a brooder box as soon as they are dry. The brooder box should be built of plywood, masonite, or a rugged cardboard and should be 36 inches long, 20 inches wide, and 24 inches high (90 × 50 × 60 cm). The box should be warmed with a heat lamp.

If wild ducklings are being raised, the top of the brooder box has to be covered with chicken wire because even tiny ducklings can jump very high and are amazingly good at climbing up the corners of a box. Ducklings of hole-nesting species, such as wood and mandarin ducks, have tiny, sharp claws, which enable them to climb up the walls of the tree holes where they were born so that they can jump to the ground. The walls of a wooden box or vertical wire mesh therefore are not much of an obstacle for them.

Need for Warmth: During the first few weeks of life most ducklings need a lot of warmth. Only the young of a few species of diving ducks are an exception because they are covered with thick, woolly down. All other ducklings should be raised in a room that is 86°F (30°C). The temperature inside the brooder box should be 90° to 95°F (32°–35°C). Measure the warmth the heat lamp emits at the distance where the ducklings are, and make sure that the ducklings have a chance to get away from the rays of the heat lamp. The bottom of the brooder box has to be warm, too. This is accomplished by placing an electric heating unit, like the ones used to keep food warm, underneath the brooder box.

As the ducklings grow older they need less heat. By the second week, 77°F (25°C) is warm enough, and after that, the temperature can be lowered even faster than for baby chickens. By the time they are four weeks old, ducklings no longer need any artificial heat, even at night, as long as the weather is warm.

Sanitation: Line the brooder box with a thick layer of absorbent paper or sheets for the first days. Keep changing the paper or cloths frequently because the digestion of tiny ducklings works quickly. Meticulous cleanliness is important. Also remove any left-over or spilled food because fungi can develop on it, and if the ducklings inhale fungal spores they may get sick and die (see Aspergillosis, page 44).

No Single Ducklings: Never try to raise a single duckling. It is the nature of ducklings to miss their siblings more than their mother. Try to have a flock of birds that are approximately of the same size and age. If there are some that are younger and smaller, they are often pushed away from the feeder by the bigger ones and thus remain weak and stunted.

Swimming Opportunity: Since the plumage of ducklings hatched in an incubator isn't water repellent, drinking water should be offered to these ducklings in shallow dishes for the first two or three days. In the second week they may be given a swimming basin with ½ inch (1 cm) of water in it. At about two weeks the plumage begins to become water resistant and the ducklings produce enough oil in their uropygial glands to take care of the entire plumage (see Dry Plumage, page 42).

Ducklings that are to be raised for market should not be allowed to swim but should get only enough water for bathing.

Natural Rearing

If you let a mother duck of an ornamental species brood and raise her own ducklings you will witness some wonderful scenes from animal life. Unfortunately, however, the number of predators interested in a tasty meal of duckling is large, and in most cases the ducklings are gone in a few days. The only alternative is to have the ducks breed and raise their young in an aviary (see Keeping Ducks in an Aviary, page 33).

Using a muscovy, a call duck, or a high-nesting flying duck as foster mother for ornamental baby ducklings is comparable in every respect to letting the natural mother brood them.

Chickens are hardly ever used anymore to chaperone ducklings once they have hatched, but broody chickens still come in handy for incubating duck eggs until they are almost ready to hatch, at which time they are moved to an incubator (see Chickens as Foster Mothers, page 50).

Commercial Uses of Ducks

Meat

Today, domestic ducks are raised almost exclusively for their meat. By contrast, the production of eggs and down is no longer of any economic significance. In recent years the per-capita consumption of poultry has risen dramatically, not only because modern consumers like the taste of poultry but also because they have become aware of the nutritional qualities of poultry. Duck meat is tender, tasty, easily digestible, and high in protein.

Fattening Young Ducks: To make the most of the natural early growth spurt and protein production of ducks, duck growers have moved the fattening period more and more ahead into the first couple of months. Almost all the roast ducks sold are young birds. When the consumer purchases a duck, he or she expects to get a bird with plenty of breast meat, well-muscled legs, and a generally lean carcass. There should be only a minimum of visible fat accumulation, such as belly fat. As a result of planned, selective breeding, many of our domestic ducks now have more muscle meat on the breast than on all the rest of the body.

Butchering

The best time to butcher young meat ducks is at nine to ten weeks. By that time the muscles are fully developed. The birds weigh 5 to 5½ pounds (2.2–2.5 kg), and haven't yet started their juvenile molt. This last factor is an important one because plucking after slaughter is made much more difficult once lots of new feathers have begun to sprout (see The Molt, a Time of Vulnerability, page 67).

Caution: If you have never butchered animals before, you should definitely consult an expert. Animal-welfare legislation requires that anyone butchering animals have the "necessary knowledge and skills" for the task. If you are lacking in this area, almost any breeder will probably be happy to provide you with sources of information. If you fail to conform to regulations you may be guilty of cruelty toward animals.

Recent animal welfare regulations prescribe that warm-blooded animals be stunned before they are bled. A good way to do this is to get a firm hold on the bird's wings with one hand and to knock the duck out with a quick, well-aimed blow on the head with a wooden club. Immediately slit the throat just below the head, slicing all the way through to the spinal chord with a single cut of a sharp knife. Let the blood drain from the suspended body. When the carcass is bled, the innards are removed through an incision made from the tip of the breastbone to the vent, but be careful not to cut into the intestines. Reach into the body cavity with your hand to loosen and pull out the internal organs. Save the heart, liver, and gizzard, and dispose of the rest of the viscera. The danger of salmonella contamination has already been mentioned in the chapter "Health Care and Diseases" (see page 40).

Dressed Weight

The usable carcass, which includes the neck, wings and edible internal organs, makes up the dressed weight. In ducks this is about 74% to 75% of the live weight. The head, feet, blood, and feathers are considered waste.

Plucking

If you have only a few birds to pluck either for your own consumption or for sale, you will probably do the job by hand. Large, commercial operations use machines that first dry-pick the birds and then strip the carcasses of the last remains of feathers with picking wax. To get rid of the pin feathers on hand-plucked birds, the carcass is singed briefly over a flame. Collecting plucked duck feathers is no longer worthwhile if you have just a few birds because duck feathers and down are imported cheaply and in large quantities from the Far East.

Storage

Most slaughtered ducks are frozen before sale. The freezing should be done immediately after butchering in a freezer with an average freezing capacity of at least 3/8 inch (1 cm) per hour. The carcasses should be frozen all the way through to 0°F (–18°C) or colder and should be kept at that temperature.

Sale

The sale of poultry is subject to many regulations that you should be familiar with ahead of slaughtering time. Consult breeders or poultry magazines (see Useful Addresses, page 93) for marketing strategies. Obviously some keepers of ducks also sell directly to consumers, but they are still subject to state regulations.

Eggs

Domestic ducks lay quite a few more eggs than do their wild relatives, the mallards, from which they are descended. Mallards lay only between 7 and 11 eggs a year, whereas the high-nesting flying duck, a breed that is genetically not very far removed from the mallard, produces 30 to 36. Heavy- and medium-weight breeds lay 80 to 130 eggs a year, and breeds developed exclusively for laying, like the Indian runner and the Campbell duck, accomplish an impressive production of up to 200 eggs a year.

The development of highly productive laying ducks and the realization that duck eggs can play a versatile role in human nutrition led to a significant increase in the number of laying ducks raised in the 1920s and 1930s. But when more and more cases of sickness following the consumption of improperly cooked duck eggs became known and it was established that salmonella bacteria consumed in the eggs were the cause of sickness, special regulations controlling the sale of duck eggs were issued. As a result, the consumption of duck eggs dropped dramatically, and no longer plays an economically significant role in the food industries of most European and American countries.

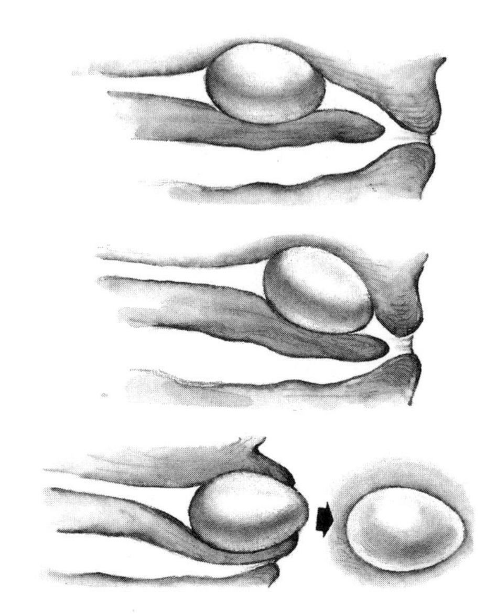

The laying of the egg. The vaginal wall is pushed through the cloaca and outside to protect the new egg from contact with excreta.

Egg Formation and Egg Laying

Female birds have functioning sexual organs only on the left side of the body. Their reproductive system consists of an ovary and an oviduct.

The ovary, which looks somewhat like a cluster of minute grapes, contains 1,100 to 1,600 egg cells when a duck reaches sexual maturity. These cells start out microscopically small, but some of them, under hormonal stimulation, start to accumulate yolk and become enlarged. They are then called ovarian follicles, though they are sometimes also referred to simply as ova.

The oviduct is a long, tubelike organ through which the ovum passes in the process of developing into a complete egg. We distinguish between different parts of the oviduct on the basis of the part they play in the formation of the egg. At the top there is the infundibulum, a funnel-shaped opening; then comes the main section, the albumen-secreting region; this is followed by the isthmus, the uterus, and, finally, the vagina.

After ovulation, that is, when the mature follicle is released from the ovary, the ovum enters the infundibulum, the funnel-like free end of the oviduct, which lies directly beneath the ovary. Fertilization occurs at this point, assuming copulation has taken place and male gametes are present. The ovum is then moved downward in the oviduct by wavelike muscle contractions (see Egg-Binding, page 44). In the next section, the albumen-secreting region, there are glands that contribute 40% to 50% of the egg's total amount of egg white.

Shell formation is the next part of the process. Now the egg—the ovum has developed far enough so that the term egg is more appropriate from this point on—enters a narrow passage in the oviduct, the isthmus, where it absorbs the remaining 50% of its albumen as well as its two-layered shell membrane. Later on an air chamber will form between the inner and the outer membranes. In the uterine section of the oviduct, calcium produced by glands in the oviduct's walls is deposited on the outside of the egg to make a hard shell. Finally, as the egg is about to emerge from the oviduct, it is covered with a secretion from the vagina. This coating dries and hardens only after the egg is laid, forming a skin that seals the pores in the shell, making it impermeable to germs.

When the egg is ready to be laid, the vagina is pushed forward until it protrudes through the cloaca. This protects the egg from contact with bacteria. The laying only takes a few minutes, and the entire process from ovulation to newly laid egg is accomplished in about 24 hours.

Properties

A duck egg differs from a chicken egg by its smooth shell that has a dull sheen to it and feels almost oily to the touch.

Weight varies. Eggs of wild mallard ducks average only 1.8 ounces (52.5 g), while eggs of domestic breeds weigh as much as 2.5 ounces (70 g).

Color can also vary. In addition to the familiar white duck eggs, there are often greenish ones, and the eggs of Rouen, Pomeranian, and East Indie ducks are often dark green or bluish green.

Fat content is 14.5%, compared to 11.6% for chicken eggs.

Yolk is pale yellow, if the ducks have been fed primarily potatoes, meals, and grains. If there is more animal protein in their diet, the yolks are lemon to dark yellow. Ducks that have been ranging free and have eaten a lot of acorns sometimes lay eggs with dark-brown yolks.

Taste hardly differs from that of chicken eggs. Occasionally duck eggs have a slightly unpleasant rancid or musty taste if the ducks have been eating too many worms, grubs, and snails when foraging. But if the birds have been getting mostly grain, their eggs taste delicious and almost sweet.

Cooking properties differ from those of chicken eggs. When whipped, the whites of duck eggs do not become as fluffy as those of chicken eggs, nor do they remain as stiff. Also, the white of a duck egg does not become as firm when cooked.

Understanding Ducks

Ducks are among some of the world's most adaptable birds. They have learned to live in the Arctic tundra as well as along the rivers of steamy, hot rain forests; on inland streams with white-water rapids as well as on the cold, stormy islands along the Antarctic. There are probably few other bird families on our planet that have succeeded in finding niches for themselves in such a variety of different habitats. In order to survive, the ducks of course had to adapt to the different environmental conditions they found, and in the process a number of genera, species, and subspecies evolved. At present some authorities recognize 37 species of dabbling ducks, 14 species of perching ducks, 15 species of diving ducks, 7 species of mergansers, 5 species of sea ducks, and 9 species of stifftail ducks.

Since most ducks are gregarious and coexist peacefully outside of the breeding season, it is possible to keep birds of different species together on the same body of water. This almost unique opportunity to observe a number of related bird species interact in a limited area was noticed early by naturalists, who started taking advantage of it toward the end of the last century. Their observations and reports have provided important groundwork for the modern science of ethology, the study of animal behavior. The study of duck behavior has yielded results that are both fascinating and surprising, and they form the subject matter of this chapter, which is intended to help the reader gain a better understanding of these interesting birds.

How Ducks Get Their Food

Dabbling Ducks: Ducks like the familiar mallard are called dabbling ducks. This means that they find their food in the water as well as on land. As they swim, they grab floating food items from the surface of the water, pick off plant particles, and sift through the mud at the bottom of shallow waters, straining out tiny food organisms with their bills. When they feed at the bottom, they "upend"—that is, they tip their bodies forward so that the front half is submerged while the back end sticks up in the air. They stay balanced in this position by treading water. Just about everybody has probably at some point seen ducks "stand on their heads" this way.

Dabbling ducks can feed on the bottom of waters up to 19 inches (48 cm) deep and stay underwater an average of 4.2 seconds at a time. They submerge their entire bodies only when they sense danger or when taking a vigorous bath. However, young mallards between the ages of four and seven weeks dive quite commonly.

Diving Ducks: Certain duck varieties get almost all their food by diving. Tufted ducks sometimes dive down as far as 40 feet (12 m). Diving ducks look for food such as mussels, clams, snails, and worms on the bottom of the water.

Deep diving is not easy for ducks because they are very light-bodied. There is always a strong force pushing them toward the surface of the water. How do they overcome it? In order to increase their specific gravity, ducks exhale before taking the plunge and press their feathers close to the body. Before actually diving, a duck tosses its head back and pulls its feet upward and forward, which makes the back end of the rump dip deeper into the water. Now comes the actual "dive." The head is thrust forward into the water, and the feet push back hard at the same time. Once underwater, the ducks press their wings close to the body. The wings are used only for increasing speed when fleeing from a danger.

When ducks dive in search of food, they propel themselves downward with even motions of their webbed feet. The higher up the feet are, the steeper the dive. When the feet are held lower, the body glides in an almost horizontal position and at a slight downward tilt. As soon as the paddling motions of the feet stop and the head is raised, the duck shoots to the water's surface like a cork. The records for staying underwater longest are held by tufted ducks with 41 seconds for the drake and 36.8 seconds for the female.

Feeding on Land: Ducks forage not only in the water but also on land. The mallard is one kind of duck that likes to feed on young grass and tender leaves as it grazes. It is adept at stripping grass seeds from their panicles and swallows acorns, beechnuts, and berries whole. It also eats insects, snails, and other small creatures—in short, anything it runs across that its bill can handle. Pieces of stale bread cannot be swallowed as is but have to be carried to the water first and softened before they are ingested.

Sometimes you may see young ducks leap up and race across the water this way and that. They are catching tiny insects, which make up their main fare during the first couple of weeks. When there are big hatches of mayflies or mosquitoes, grown ducks, remembering their youthful ways, can be seen performing these acrobatic feats, too.

A Duck's Bill, the Perfect Sieve

Ducks sift the mud at the bottom of shallow waters through their bills and eat the tiny organisms that live there. They couldn't do this if their bills weren't highly specialized for this task. The broad, flattened upper mandible is covered with soft skin that has many sensitive tastebuds distributed over it, particularly near the tip. The nerves leading to the tastebuds run through tiny pores or canals in the bone of the mandible. Because of this, the tactile sense is extremely sensitive in the bill and makes it easy for ducks to sense and catch tiny organisms in cloudy water and mud.

Straining: Along the outer edge of the lower mandible as well as on the inner edge of the protruding upper mandible there are many fine parallel horny plates, called lamellae, arranged in a comblike pattern. The tongue is fringed with similar lamellae along the sides. When a duck picks up a mouthful of mud, it closes its bill and pushes the water out with the tongue, forcing it out between the lamellae. Solid matter is retained, and the water is strained out. The sensitive tongue quickly distinguishes what is edible, and the inedible mud particles are discarded.

When a duck sifts through organic matter floating on the water's surface, the tongue serves as a sucking mechanism. It draws a stream of water in at the tip of the bill and lets it flow out through the lamellae at the back of the bill, where usable food particles are caught.

At the tip of the upper mandible there is a small hook, which is called the nail. It is the only part of the bill with a tough, hard skin, and it serves to get a secure hold on big pieces of food as well as on slippery pieces.

How Ducks Bathe

The bathing ritual, as we may rightly call it, almost always consists of a definite sequence of motions. First the duck dips its head into the water and splashes water over its back with sideward motions of the head. While the water flows down the back, the tail is spread and one or both wings lifted with repeated fanning of the primaries. This phase of the ritual may last for 10 minutes or more. Then the duck lowers its breast deep into the water, often while pulling its head in close to its body. At the same time the body tilts more or less to the side and every so often rolls over in a sideways somersault.

When the duck has regained its normal swimming position, it starts "beating its wings." What this means is that the duck beats down hard on the water first with one wing and then with the other.

This phase of the ritual is followed by the most eye-catching activity, namely a period of wild dashing across the water and diving. Once one duck starts doing this, others often follow. After diving several times with open wings, the ducks scoot across the water, wings flapping wildly, take to the air briefly, and then plunge back into the water. They move around on the water this way for some time, splashing, diving, and flying with such vigor

The bathing ritual consists of a definite sequence of body movements as described in the section "How Ducks Bathe" (on page 63).

that a casual observer might easily interpret the action as aggressive chases. In fact, the ducks are simply indulging in one of their favorite pastimes, namely, bathing.

Ducks take full baths like this, which can last 10 to 20 minutes, once or twice a day when the weather is sunny. On overcast days they usually don't bathe at all. Between baths, ducks keep themselves clean by pulling their wing, tail, and flank feathers through their bills quickly and forcefully. The birds often scratch themselves, too.

Preening, a Crucial Activity

When you watch a duck preening itself meticulously and almost endlessly, you might think all this fussy care of the plumage a bit excessive. But keeping the feathers in top condition is crucial to survival, for the plumage has to keep out cold and wetness. To function effectively, the feathers have to be properly arranged and oiled at regular, short intervals, a task that is taken care of after bathing (see page 65).

When a duck leaves the water, its first concern is to dry its plumage. Shaking the body makes drops of water fly off in all directions and causes the feathers to settle in their proper places. The process starts with the tail, which is shaken vigorously while the small contour feathers are raised; then the shaking moves forward over the slightly raised body all the way to the neck. At the same time the wings vibrate in place, and the raised head rotates several times, the bill describing a circle.

Ducks also scratch themselves with their bills and toes. Probably this helps get moisture out of the deeper layers of the plumage. All these preening motions help the barbules interlock with microscopically small hooks so that the feathers stay in place and are properly fluffed up. This way enough air is trapped in the plumage so that it continues to serve as a warm insulating coat covering the entire body.

Beating the water with the wings. In the course of the bathing ritual, ducks "beat their wings." They hit the water first with one wing, then with the other.

The Function of the Oil Gland

When the feathers are dry enough, the duck begins to oil them. First it rubs its chin, cheek, and crown over the bared oil gland just above the tail. Then the wing and the tail feathers are quickly drawn through the bill. In this process the bill itself and the entire hind part of the body also get greased. Working this way, a duck can pick up oil from the gland up to seven times within five minutes, reaching back alternately on the right and left side.

The females of some duck species stop oiling their plumage when they settle down on their eggs and don't start again until just before the ducklings are due to hatch. This freshly distributed oil is automatically transferred from the mother's feathers to the down of the newborn ducklings. Ducklings do have oil glands that are functional at birth, and the behavior of oiling the feathers is inborn, but apparently the glands aren't productive enough at first, so that the mother has to help out (see Dry Plumage, page 42).

Ducks Need Rest and Sleep, Too

All vertebrates need periods of rest and sleep of various length. Ducks are diurnal as well as nocturnal, alternating periods of activity lasting roughly 45 to 75 minutes with rest periods of about 30 to 45 minutes. Ducks are most quiescent in the middle of the day and most active at night and in the early morning hours. Ducks that live in captivity have learned to change their routine because they are fed during the day and have to eat the food quickly before free-flying birds, like crows, gulls, city pigeons, and sparrows get to it.

Wild ducks that are not confined, however, behave like all wild birds and adhere to a definite routine if they live in a natural environment and without human interference. They rest or sleep from about 9 to 11 o'clock in the morning, bathe and preen themselves around noon, and spend most of the afternoon resting. At dusk they get more active, and most of the night and into the forenoon of the next day they are busy searching for food.

Wild ducks spend their resting periods and their feeding periods in different waters. They usually fly from their resting quarters to their feeding waters after sunset and return in the morning. The nightly foraging is interrupted by short rest periods. When it is too dark to see, they rely on their acute organs of taste and touch perception in the tongue and the skin of the bill. Since most inland water frequented by ducks is opaque, sight is of no great use in dabbling or diving for food.

Mallards and other dabbling ducks often spend the night on inland fields and meadows far from bodies of water. Here they are safe from raptors and hunters, and all they have to watch out for are foxes and martens. In the open country they can escape these enemies by flying straight up in the air.

Rest Positions: Ducks on land rest either by

sitting on the ground or by standing on one leg. But they always keep a sharp eye on their surroundings. Since several of them often rest together, at least one of them can always keep guard. On the water, resting ducks let themselves drift with their bills tucked deep into the innermost feathers of the second wing segment. One leg is usually resting, pulled up next to the body, while the other paddles every so often to keep the body moving in the same direction.

We know very little about actual sleep in ducks. But we can assume with some degree of certainty that short periods of light sleep alternate with periods of wakefulness, and we are probably safe in asserting that wild ducks cannot afford a deep sleep.

Escape From Enemies

Ducks resting or foraging on land head for the water as quickly as they can if they sense danger. Since they are able to rise straight up into the air, they have not much trouble getting away from predators like foxes, dogs, cats, and martens. When they are pursued in the water, dabbling ducks like our familiar mallard can dive out of sight just as fast as true diving ducks. When they dive to get away from some danger, ducks use their wings underwater for speed, abruptly change direction, and surface again in unexpected places where their enemies are not likely to look for them.

In heavily settled areas like central Europe, there are very few animal predators left that can attack ducks. Sea eagles have become so rare that they no longer represent a threat. If they do hunt ducks, they follow their diving and surfacing prey until it finally tires and can then be gripped easily.

Diversionary Behavior: Like many mother birds, female ducks try to divert a predator's attention away from their young. A duck mother feigns lameness and injury hoping to distract the enemy. Fluttering and reeling, she lures the predator away from the nest by drawing attention to herself. Then she suddenly makes her escape by taking off into the air.

Social Behavior

Ducks are extremely sociable birds when they are not engaged in breeding and rearing young. It is this sociable quality that makes them so suitable for captivity. The various species that winter in Europe often gather together in huge aggregations consisting of thousands of pairs and some unattached birds that try to join the crowd. These aggregations dissolve again with the arrival of spring weather, when pairs take off for their breeding grounds.

How Ducks Survive Our Winter

If you see ducks swimming in open water surrounded by ice and snow or resting on lumps of ice, you may wonder how these birds manage to stand the cold and stay alive. Cold winters are, of course, hard on the birds, and weak ones fail to survive.

Healthy ducks get ready for winter in the fall, putting on a subcutaneous layer of fat to keep them warm. A plumage that is in good shape and well maintained makes an additional insulating coat that protects the animals against hypothermia. When the wings are closed, they are often tucked into a kind of pocket formed by the feathers on the side of the breast, where they are protected from the water. But what about the feet and the delicate skin that forms the webs between the toes? These webs are not at all insensitive to the cold. That is why ducks usually paddle with only one foot at a time when swimming in very cold water. The resting foot is tucked into a feather pocket, as into a fur muff, and it emerges only when the first foot has gotten too cold and needs warming up. Ducks that originally come from tropical regions often freeze their feet and webs if an inexperienced caretaker lets them swim in icy water (see Important Signs of Sickness, page 41). When ducks rest on a cold surface, such as an ice floe, they usually lower themselves onto the belly. This way the feet can warm up in the thick abdominal plumage.

It is also much harder to find sufficient food in the winter than during the warmer seasons. It has been observed, however, that healthy mallards, for instance, can survive up to two weeks without eating, and in most situations this is probably enough time for the birds to locate waters with a better food supply.

The Molt, a Time of Vulnerability

Birds replace their feathers during the molt. In ducks, molting is a rather complicated process that takes place in separate stages. The down the nestlings are born with begins to be replaced by small contour feathers at 3 weeks. At the same time the big flight feathers begin to grow in. At 4 weeks the breast is covered with feathers, and a few weeks later the flight feathers are in place. In mallards this stage is reached at 7½ weeks; in Pekin ducks, a domestic breed, not until 8 to 10 weeks. But by then Pekin ducks are already much too heavy to fly and are therefore earthbound. If they are raised as market ducklings, they are slaughtered shortly before the juvenile molt is completed because new feathers growing in are very difficult to pluck (see page 42).

Drakes, both wild and domestic, undergo an additional molt in the summer. In this molt they lose their nuptial plumage and put on a duller coat of feathers which renders them rather similar to the females and is called the "eclipse" plumage. This camouflage plumage is very useful because soon the drakes will shed all their flight feathers simultaneously and be flightless for three to four weeks. After August they undergo a new molt, which restores their nuptial splendor.

With the onset of the molt, the drakes leave their mates and the breeding grounds. They take off in the early summer, before the flight feathers begin to molt, and sometimes cover long distances to reach large bodies of open water where they join many other drakes to molt together. In migratory species,

A wire cage for catching ducks. Ornamental ducks kept on large ponds should get used to getting fed in such a cage in the fall. When the water freezes over, you can catch them in the cage and take them to an aviary with an attached shelter where they can winter over.

the drakes band together to fly to their winter territories.

Wild female ducks cannot afford to molt their flight feathers so early because they are still brooding and rearing their young when the drakes take off to molt. Females don't shed their flight feathers until the young ducklings can fly.

Being unable to fly for weeks is of course a highly dangerous situation for birds. That is why dabbling ducks become extremely shy during this period and hide in dense vegetation growing along the edges of water. Diving ducks, on the other hand, which rely on diving out of sight even when they can fly, feel safest on wide, open waters during their molting period.

The Reproductive Period

Courtship Behavior

The courtship rituals of ducks are exceptionally fascinating. We will discuss them here, using the mallard duck as an example.

Mated drakes already start their courtship displays in the fall. Often a group of them will congregate on the water for a communal display, which the females, having gathered around the group, watch. The display starts with the drake raising the feathers of the head and pulling in the neck while the tail is shaken repeatedly. Then the head is lifted and tossed from side to side with increasing vigor with the bill dipping into the water. Suddenly the body is jerked forward, the head lowered, and drops of water are thrown up by the bill, which sweeps rapidly back and forth across the water. Before the body resumes its normal position on the water, the duck emits a high whistle. This display is called the "grunt-whistle" and is always accompanied by tail shaking.

In another phase of the display, all the drakes in a courtship group often emit a long whistled note together at the same time while lifting their heads high and then lowering them. At the same time the fanned tails are lifted high, which makes the drakes' bodies look strangely short and squat. The tips of the wings are pointing straight up and the secondaries are pressed upward. Seen from the side and in this posture the drakes prominently display the tips of their wings and the curly feathers in the middle of the tail, the so-called "sex feathers." This curious stance is maintained for only a few seconds; then the drakes drop back to their normal posture but still keep their heads and necks raised.

Unattached drakes point their bills at any female that happens to be close, whereas bonded males address their display exclusively to their chosen mates. A bonded male will swim back and forth around his mate in semicircles, extending his head forward low over the water while nodding vigorously. This display is called "nod-swimming."

Then the drake raises his head again and turns the back of the neck with its bright green plumage toward the courted female. This is called the "turning-of-the-back-of-the-head." In the "down-up" phase, which follows next, the breast is immersed deep into the water before the head shoots up high and the bill raises a fountain of water drops. When the head is in its highest position, the courting drake whistles and then calls "raeb-raeb" with the bill tilted upward.

How Partners Get Acquainted with Each Other

Mallard females take a much more active part in wooing a potential mate than the males do. An unattached drake joining a group of females is therefore in the enviable position of being able to chose and reject as he likes.

Females ready to pick partners swim toward unattached drakes and display "inciting" behavior. When inciting, a female approaches a drake that appeals to her and at the same time makes threatening gestures across her shoulder toward any strange drake that happens to be swimming around in the vicinity. She will go through these motions even if the strange drake is not in the direction her gestures

"Inciting" is the most common love declaration female ducks address to the drakes of their choice. When she incites, the female turns toward her chosen drake and at the same time makes threatening motions across her shoulder at some other drake.

are pointing toward. The threatening gestures are accompanied by a series of "gagg" notes that sound somewhat like the bleating of goats. The threatening and calling is done with the head and back feathers flattened down smoothly.

"Inciting" is the most common and widespread form of love declaration among ducks. It is used by females first as a marriage proposal and later as a demonstrative affirmation of belonging to the drake. If, in the courtship ritual, the unattached drake to whom the inciting was addressed responds by chasing the indicated strange drake away, this is a sign that he is accepting the female's overtures and is willing to "become engaged."

How an "Engaged" Pair Behaves

If the drake has taken a liking to the female—as his chasing away the strange drake indicates—he will stay close to her, drink to her, and pretend to preen himself. In pretend preening, or "preening-behind-the-wing," the drake raises his wings up at an angle to display the metallic green speculum on the wing and runs his bill over the edge of the secondaries, creating an audible rasping noise that sounds something like "rrrrp." Then the two partners swim away from each other in opposite directions, and all contact between them seems to come to an end. But whenever they meet again they go through the motions just described, reaffirming their commitment to each other. Things can go on like this for days and weeks until the drake begins to follow the female around.

Now the two often have long tête-à-têtes during which she drinks to him and he returns the compliment, pretend-preens, and utters "raep-raep" calls. If a strange drake approaches at this point, the female strongly incites her "suitor" to drive the intruder away as a demonstration of their commitment to each other. If he does her bidding, the bond between the pair can be regarded as established. Such bonds, as well as firm pair formations, can take place any time from the end of August until winter.

Matrimony

"Married" ducks can be recognized in a winter flock by the fact that they spend more time near each other and stay closer together than the rest of the birds. They make threatening gestures toward other ducks, sometimes go off by themselves, and are generally inseparable. They rest huddled close together, behave as equals when feeding, and the male defends his mate if another drake happens to come too close. When the two partners get separated, the lost one keeps calling until they are reunited. When they leave the water in the spring, the female takes to the air first, while in the fall the drake takes the initiative.

Matings take place as early as the fall even though the gamete-producing glands are not yet active at this time. Presumably these matings serve to strengthen the pair bond. The actual mounting or "treading" is always preceded by mutual "head-pumping." One partner suddenly moves the head down in several jerky movements, keeping the bill horizontal, and then slowly raises it to its initial position. Then both partners start head-pumping, which becomes more and more intense until the female is lying flat on the water. The drake now climbs onto her back, grabs the feathers on her nape with his bill, and pushes her into the water so deep that she is often almost entirely submerged. Then he presses his tail against the female's lifted tail from the side, and copulation takes place as the pair moves back and forth rhythmically.

Since the drake has a kind of penis, the pair is able to stay locked together during copulation, which always takes place in the water. A few

Ducks mate almost exclusively in the water. When a drake mounts his mate, he grabs the feathers on her nape and pushes her down until she is almost completely submerged.

domestic ducks are also able to mate on the gound, but the fertilization rate under these conditions is often not as satisfactory.

As soon as the drake stops treading, he draws his head way back and emits a sharp whistle. Then he nod-swims around the female in a big circle, after which both start bathing and preening themselves while beating their wings.

Pursuit Chases in the Spring

In the spring one often sees a single flying female duck pursued by several drakes. What happens is that a strange drake tries to get hold of a female duck's tail by biting it, and the female's mate tries to do the same to the stranger. Such chases can go on for 3,000 feet (1,000 m) or so. They get started when mated drakes whose partners are brooding are trying to rape other females.

Even ducks that are brooding or leading their young are not safe from such pursuits by one or more drakes, but the chase is usually unsuccessful. When it is enacted on land, one gets a chance to observe the "gesture of repulsion" clearly. The female approaches the drakes with raised head and back feathers, holding ther head way back on her shoulders, and utters several sharp "gaek" calls with wide open bill.

In animal parks it happens not infrequently that pinioned females, unable to escape from males whose wings have not been tampered with, are drowned when several drakes try to mount them.

Nest-Building and Incubation

The drake and his mate select the nest site together, but the female does all the nest building. She pokes the ground with her bill in the spot that has been selected, then lowers her breast onto it and makes swimming motions with her feet to scrape leaves and loose earth toward the back. In this way a shallow hole is gradually formed, which is smoothed out by the pressure of the breast as the duck slowly rotates in it. Only what is within reach of the bill is incorporated in the nest. Ducks do not carry nesting materials to the nest site.

When the female leaves the nest after she has started laying eggs, she heaps nesting material over the incomplete clutch and uses her bill to bury the eggs in the material. She waits until the clutch is complete before plucking down from her breast, which she distributes in a circle around the clutch. When she does this, she selects feathers that match the colors of the surroundings so that the clutch is well camouflaged.

When hatching time approaches and the female hears the first chirping of the chicks inside their shells, she changes her incubating behavior. She turns the eggs much more frequently than before and emits soft calls herself. In this way the ducklings are imprinted with the voice of their mother before they are even born. When an enemy approaches, the mother gives warning calls, and the chirping stops. Shortly before the actual hatching the mother begins to oil her plumage thoroughly, so that the down of the newly hatched ducklings can absorb some of the secretion of the mother's oil gland and become water repellent right away (see Dry Plumage, page 42). The shells left behind by the hatchlings are mostly eaten by the mother, and the baby ducklings leave the nest for good 6 to 12 hours after hatching. Ducks are nidifugous birds, which means that they are able to take care of themselves and leave the nest soon after birth.

The Duck Mother and Her Babies

In dabbling ducks the family attachment is quite close and lasts longer than in diving ducks. A mallard mother broods her ducklings for three to four weeks. Compared to chickens, ducklings need much less warmth from their mother because their thick down coat protects them against the cold.

The mother doesn't feed her ducklings, nor does she teach them how to find food. She simply goes to places where she knows that there is abundant food. All the ducklings follow her single file, each copying exactly what the one in front is doing.

Sibling Cohesion: The fact that ducklings stick primarily to each other and that the attachment to the mother is secondary makes them rather unique among baby birds. It doesn't matter if the mother is out of sight for most of them when she leads them. Even if the mother dies, this does not necessarily spell doom for the ducklings. The young of the tufted duck, for instance, fend for themselves when they are just a few days old and can, if the weather is not too bad, survive their mother's death within the first two weeks in spite of cold nights.

Mallard ducklings make their first flying attempts at seven and a half weeks and are fully able to fly by the time they are eight weeks old. At this point, the bond between parent birds and their young dissolves completely.

Baby ducklings follow their mother single file. Each copies every move of the one in front and faithfully follows all detours around obstacles.

Ornamental Ducks and Utility Ducks

In the following descriptions the most popular ornamental ducks and utility breeds are introduced. The ornamental ducks fall into two groups, the dabbling ducks and the diving ducks, while utility or commercial ducks are usually divided into heavyweight, medium-weight, and lightweight breeds.

The following descriptions of species and breeds contain information on origin, appearance, habitat, requirements in captivity, breeding, egg-laying, rate of growth, and weight of the ducks. The sizes given for wild or ornamental ducks indicate the length of an adult bird, measured from the tip of the bill to the tip of the tail.

Ornamental Ducks: Dabbling Ducks

Dabbling ducks, such as the mallard, can be recognized by how high they ride on the water and by the placement of the legs close to the middle of the body. Dabbling ducks feed in shallow water, frequently upending to seek food at the bottom.

Mallard Duck

Anas platyrhynchos

Size: 23 inches (58 cm)
Origin: Northern to central Eurasia; North America, especially in the Mississippi Valley. Has been introduced into parts of Australia and New Zealand.
Description: The drake has an iridescent bottle-green head marked off by a white neck ring, a chocolate brown breast, a black rear end including the tail coverts, and a dark blue speculum. The tail is white with four curled feathers in the middle, called sex feathers. The bill is yellowish green; the legs, orange-red. The female is mostly brown and has an olive-green bill.

On the waters of city parks one often finds mallards whose blood is mixed with that of domesticated mallards. These birds tend to have differently colored plumage. The neck ring of the male is often absent, and white feathers are intermixed with the colors.
Habitat: Mallards live on all kinds of water but clearly prefer shallow lakes and ponds with an abundance of organic matter to feed on.
Captivity: The mallard is the largest wild duck found in Europe and arguably the most beautiful of all wild ducks. It is the stock from which all our domestic breeds with the exception of the muscovy duck are descended.

Mallards exist in large numbers and are extremely adaptable. They will settle on even the tiniest pond. If you have a small, ornamental garden pond with some water and marsh plants, you can almost count on a pair of mallards arriving in the spring on the look-out for a nesting site. Mallards living on ornamental duck ponds are often rather quarrelsome, and if their flight is not restrained they tend to interbreed with related species, such as the spotbill duck. Raising purebred mallards is therefore possible only in an aviary. Since wild mallards seek out garden ponds on their own, there is generally little reason to clip their wings. Mallards are known to have lived as long as 22 to 29 years in captivity.
Breeding: Breeding mallards is easy. The birds accept just about any nest site that is offered. The breeding season begins any time after mid-February, depending on the climate. A clutch consists of 7 to 11 eggs, which can be white, yellowish, grayish green, or light green. Incubation lasts 28 days. Rearing the ducklings is unproblematic; they start flying at 7½ weeks and reach sexual maturity before they are one year old.

Spotbilled Duck

Anas poecilorhyncha

Size: 23½ inches (60 cm)
Origin: Indian peninsula, Sri Lanka, Burma, Korea, China, Mongolia, Southeastern Siberia, and Japan.
Description: The two sexes differ only slightly in

appearance. The crown is dark brown, the head and neck are grayish white, and a band across the eyes is brown. The back and shoulder feathers are dark brown with gray borders. The speculum is green and has a white patch above it. The bill, which is black, has a yellow tip, and the base of the upper mandible is red.
Habitat: Shallow lakes and ponds with lush vegetation. Resident birds.
Captivity: Spotbill ducks are attractive birds about the size of mallards that can winter over in our latitudes in spite of their tropical origins.
Breeding: Pure breeding is possible only in aviaries because spotbill ducks kept unrestrained on ponds inevitably interbreed with wild mallards. Breeding season is in mid-April. A clutch consists of 8 to 14 white, brownish, or pale green eggs, which are incubated 26 to 28 days. The birds reach sexual maturity toward the end of their first year.

Northern Pintail

Anas acuta

Size: 25½ inches (65 cm)
Origin: Northern and central Eurasia; North America.
Description: Pintails are large, slender, and long-necked. The drake is dove gray with a brown head and a white throat and breast. The white extends up the side of the head in a stripe that ends at eye height. The undertail coverts and the long, narrow, pointed tail are black. The bill and the legs are bluish gray. The female is brown and can be distinguished from other female dabbling ducks by her long, thin neck and pointed tail.
Habitat: Large lakes with plenty of vegetation in open, treeless landscapes. Migratory birds.
Captivity: The pintail is an elegant ornamental bird, lively, peaceful, winter hardy, and modest in its demands. Pintails have lived in captivity up to 20 years.
Breeding: Breeding pintails on largish ponds surrounded with dense vegation is quite easy. These ducks nest hidden in tall grass and other leafy plants, and they also accept nest houses and boxes. The breeding season starts in mid-April. A clutch consists of 7 to 11 cream-colored to greenish yellow eggs, which are incubated from 21 to 23 days. Raising the ducklings presents no problems. The young are ready to fly at 7 weeks and reach sexual maturity by the end of the year. They often do not breed until the second year.

Gadwall

Anas strepera

Size: 19¾ inches (50 cm)
Origin: Central Eurasia; North America, but rare in eastern New York and New England.
Description: The gadwall is somewhat smaller than the mallard. The drake is gray all over except for the black tail coverts and some chestnut brown on the inner wing. The bill is gray; the legs, orange-yellow. Females are predominantly brown and can be distinguished from female mallards by their yellow bills with a gray center ridge and by the white speculum.
Habitat: Large, shallow, inland waters with lush vegetation offering a plentiful food supply. Not in wooded areas. Migratory birds.
Captivity: The gadwall is an attractively colored duck that is gregarious and modest in its demands. Since it is migratory, it cannot winter over outside. It feeds primarily on vegetable matter. If a pair of birds with trimmed wings is released on the right kind of lake or pond, they may settle there. Gadwalls are faithful to their nest sites and will return there the following spring with their grown young. In captivity gadwalls can live up to 16 or 17 years.
Breeding: Breeding gadwalls is not difficult if they have a pond that is surrounded by grass and low shrubbery. They nest in dense vegetation. The breeding season is in late April to early May. A clutch consists of 8 to 12 cream-colored eggs, which are incubated 25 to 27 days. Raising the ducklings is unproblematic. The young ducks are able to fly at 7 weeks and reach sexual maturity toward the end of their first year.

Falcated Teal

Anas falcata

Size: 19 inches (48 cm)
Origin: From central Siberia to northern Japan.
Description: Falcated teals are smaller than mallards. The drake has a purplish chestnut crown and iridescent copper to bronze-colored plumage on the front of the head and the cheeks. A broad green band reaches from the eyes to the long crest at the back of the head. The throat is white with a black collar running across the white. The back and the breast have white feathers with black edges forming a scallop pattern. The wing coverts are light gray with white tips. Long, crescent-shaped, black-and-white feathers that are extended inner secondaries curve down over the hind parts on both sides of the tail. The undertail coverts are black with a large, bold, creamy yellow patch on each side. The flanks and abdomen have fine black and white barring. The female resembles the female mallard but has a thick, short crest.
Habitat: Bogs and swampy rivers running through forests. In the winter, falcated teal are found in rice fields and on inland lakes. Migratory birds.
Captivity: This is a very decorative duck that is gregarious, modest in its demands, and winter hardy. It feeds primarily on vegetable matter. If several drakes are kept, they engage in communal courtship displays in the presence of the females, which take an active part in the displays.
Breeding: Breeding these ducks is not difficult because at this point in history only birds bred in captivity are available for sale. They will breed even in garden ponds if these are well planted. The nest is built among bushes not too far from the water. Falcated teal do not accept nest houses or nest baskets. Between mid-May and mid-June 6 to 10 brownish yellow eggs are laid and incubated for 25 to 26 days. The young ducks usually start breeding when barely one year old.

The falcated teal is an extrmely attractive ornamental duck and is easy to maintain.

Northern Shoveler, Common Shoveler, European Shoveler

Anas clypeata

Size: 19¾ inches (50 cm)
Origin: Northern and central Eurasia; North America.
Description: Shovelers are the only ducks with a huge spatulate bill. The drake has a bottle-green head, a white breast, light blue inner wings, a large white area on the shoulders, and bright chestnut underparts. The bill is black and the legs orange-yellow. The female is brown but can easily be distinguished from other species by her large spoon-shaped bill.
Habitat: Shallow water with lush vegetation offering plenty of food. Migratory birds.
Captivity: A drake in his nuptial plumage is the most colorful ornamental duck and a very handsome bird. These ducks are of a peaceful disposition, but they cannot winter where it gets very cold because the lamellae of their bills ice over when the temperature drops too low. Shovelers have special nutritional demands. With their bills, which are used like sieves, they strain out tiny organisms (plankton) from the surface water. Typically several drakes form a "convoy," swimming close together one behind the other and incessantly skimming the water. These ducks need a diet high in proteins. They can live up to 19 years in captivity.

Breeding: Breeding shovelers is not difficult if you have a pond for them that is surrounded by thick grass, leafy plants, and bushes. A clutch consists of 8 to 12 grayish green or, more rarely, cream-colored eggs. Incubation lasts 25 to 27 days. Popular rearing foods are starter meal for turkeys, duckweed, and mosquito larvae. Northern shovelers reach sexual maturity at 10 to 11 months but don't breed until the second year.

European Wigeon

Anas penelope

Size: 17¾ inches (45 cm)
Origin: Northern Eurasia.
Description: The drake has a chestnut-brown head with a yellow blaze on the forehead. The body is gray with a white abdomen and black undertail coverts. The breast is a pinkish wine-red. The bill is lead gray; the legs, black. The female differs from other ornamental species by her round head, small bill, and the reddish brown color of her plumage.
Habitat: Shallow water with lush vegetation. Often found on bits of open water in the marshy meadows of the Arctic tundra. Winters along ice-free ocean bays. Migratory birds.
Captivity: The European wigeon is a decorative ornamental duck that is winter hardy, modest in its demands, and gregarious. Its call is a two-syllable whistle rendered in writing as "wa'-chew." The whistle accounts for the German name for wigeons, namely, *Pfeifente* or whistling duck. European wigeons are pure vegetarians, and they need grass to graze on. The highest age reached by this duck in captivity is 24 years.
Breeding: It is possible to breed this species on a garden pond that is surrounded by bushes and other vegetation if there is also a lawn or meadow nearby. The nest is built in shrubbery or in a nest house. The breeding season is from mid-May to early June. A clutch usually consists of 9 creamy yellow eggs that are incubated 22 to 25 days by the female. Rearing the ducklings presents no problems since the baby ducks start foraging very early. They are able to fly at six weeks and may reach sexual maturity at ten months, though often not until later.

American Wigeon (also called Baldpate)

Anas americana

Size: 18 to 22¾ inches (46–58 cm)
Origin: Alaska, Canada, western United States.
Description: The forehead and crown of the drake are white, and a broad streak of green runs from the eyes to the nape. The rest of the head and the upper throat are grayish white, delicately dotted with black. The tertials are long, broad, lance-shaped, and colored black and white. The upper parts, breast, and flanks are reddish brown, and the abdomen, white. There is also a white patch on the side of the rear end, and the tail coverts are black. The female resembles her European cousin but is paler, and her head is yellowish white mottled with brown.
Habitat: Prairie and tundra lakes and open marshland. In the winter, flooded fields and rice paddies. Migratory birds.
Captivity: Similar to the European wigeon. If kept together, American and European wigeons commonly crossbreed. The hybrid offspring look more like the European side of the family and are fertile.
Breeding: Since most of the American wigeons available are bred in captivity, breeding them is not too difficult. Nests are built underneath bushes or in nest houses. The female does not tolerate disruptions during incubation. The breeding season is in May and June, and a clutch consisting of 8 to 10 creamy white eggs hatches after 22 to 25 days of incubation. The baby ducklings are hardy, grow fast, and reach sexual maturity at 10 months.

Chiloë Wigeon

Anas sibilatrix

Size: 17¾ inches (45 cm)
Origin: From southern Brazil to Tierra del Fuego.
Description: The color pattern of the two sexes is

the same. The front of the head from the forehead to the chin is white. There is a whitish ear patch. The crown, sides of the head, and neck are black with an iridescent green sheen. The throat and crop region is barred black and white in a scale pattern. The tertials are broad, lance-shaped, and black with white edges. The wing coverts have a large white area, and the speculum is a velvety black with a metallic green sheen. The flanks are orange-brown; the abdomen and tail coverts, white; and the tail, black. The bill and the legs are lead gray.
Habitat: Shallow lakes and swamps in the pampas region. Migratory birds.
Captivity: This species is highly recommended as an ornamental duck. It is gregarious, has modest demands, and is winter hardy. Both sexes wear their colorful nuptial plumage all year round. These ducks can be kept even on small garden ponds, but they do need a grassy area for grazing.
Breeding: Chiloë wigeons are easy to breed. Set up brood houses close to the water. The drake keeps guard over the sitting female. The breeding season starts in eary April. A clutch of 6 to 11 off-white eggs hatches after 24 to 25 days of incubation. The baby ducklings are very independent and immediately start foraging. Both parents share in the care of the young, which is very unusual in dabbling ducks. Unattached drakes readily accept orphaned ducklings of other species and act as model parents for them. The young ducks acquire their adult plumage in the fall of their first year. They are sometimes ready to breed at the end of their first year but more often not until the spring of the second year.

European Green-winged Teal

Anas crecca

Size: 13¾ inches (35 cm)
Origin: Northern and central Eurasia; also, but more rarely, North America. (The male of the North American subspecies has a white mark on the side of the breast.)
Description: The green-winged teal is the smallest wild duck of the northern hemisphere. The head of the drake is chestnut brown with a broad green band running from the eye across the side of the face to the nape. Most of the rest of the plumage is delicately barred black and white, and the breast is yellowish white with black spots. There is a large creamy yellow patch bordered with black on the side of the rear end and a white shoulder stripe. The speculum is green. The female is mottled brown and buff with light-colored cheeks and underparts and a green speculum.
Habitat: Shallow inland waters with lush vegetation; also lakes in marsh areas and heaths. Migratory birds.
Captivity: This decorative duck is recommended for an aviary and garden pond. It is gregarious, modest in its demands, and winter hardy. Males engage in interesting communal courtship displays during which they utter the "krick" whistle. Two banded wild green-winged teal are known to have reached 17 years of age.
Breeding: Breeding these ducks in captivity is easy. They build nests in thick grass or other leafy plants and also accept nest boxes. The breeding season is in early May. A clutch of 6 to 12 cream-colored eggs is incubated 21 to 25 days. The baby ducklings are rather delicate and sensitive to cold and moisture. They should therefore be reared artificially in a brooder. They are able to fly at 44 days and ready to breed at the end of their first year.

Garganey or Cricket Teal

Anas querquedula

Size: 15 inches (35 cm)
Origin: Central Eurasia.
Description: The drake has a brown head and neck with a broad white band running from the eye to the nape. The brass-brown breast is sharply set off from the gray flanks, which are delicately barred with black. Long black-and-white scapulars hang down over the green speculum. The female resembles the female green-winged teal, but the colors on the head show greater contrast, and the speculum is blue.
Habitat: Shallow inland waters with lush vegeta-

tion offering plenty of food. Migratory birds.
Captivity: This duck with its rather subdued but attractive coloring is well suited to being kept in an aviary or on a garden pond. It is gregarious and modest in its demands but not quite winter hardy. Wild garganeys live up to 8 years.
Breeding: Garganeys are easy to breed on a small garden pond surrounded by dense vegetation. The breeding season is from mid-April to May. A clutch of 8 to 11 creamy yellow eggs is incubated 21 to 23 days. The females are reliable brooders and good mothers. The young ducklings are able to fly at five to six weeks and reach sexual maturity at ten months, although they usually don't breed until their second year.

Cinnamon Teal

Anas cyanoptera

Size: 14½ to 17 inches (37–43 cm)
Origin: Western North America; northwestern and southern South America.
Description: The drake is a deep chestnut brown with light blue inner wings, a green speculum, black tail coverts, a black bill, and orange-yellow legs. The female is brown with light blue inner wings and a green speculum.
Habitat: Shallow ponds with lots of vegetation, grassy marshes; in winter, lagoons and rice paddies. Migratory birds.
Captivity: This is an attractive and quiet duck suitable for an aviary or garden pond, but it sometimes does not get along well with other ducks; it is not winter-hardy and therefore needs a shelter.
Breeding: Breeding attempts in aviaries and on backyard ponds are often successful. The breeding season is from mid-April to late May. During this period, breeding pairs cannot be kept together with others of their species or with any other small ducks, such as blue-winged teal, green-winged teal, or garganeys, because the drakes are extremely aggressive. Nests are built in dense vegetation. A clutch consists of 10 to 12 white to yellowish eggs, which are incubated for 24 to 25 days. Rearing the baby ducklings is unproblematic. The young ducks are able to fly at about seven weeks and reach sexual maturity toward the end of the year.

Baikal Teal, Formosa Teal, Spectacled Teal

Anas Formosa

Size: 15¾ inches (40 cm)
Origin: Northeastern Siberia; winters in China and Japan.
Description: The head of the drake is black at the top. The dark yellow face has a crescent-shaped stripe starting behind the eye and running down the side of the neck. A black line cuts downward across the yellow cheek and curves forward, ending in a black area on the chin and throat. The breast is a pale wine-red with dark round spots, and the flanks are gray with delicate, wavy barring. The elongated, narrow scapulars taper to a point and are black along the center, yellow along the upper, and brown along the lower edge. The speculum is a bronze-green. The female resembles the female green-winged teal but has a white spot at the base of the bill.
Habitat: Ponds and rivers in the forests of the

The Baikal teal lives in the Siberian taiga. It is a beautiful small ornamental duck that is gregarious and winter-hardy.

Siberian taiga. The Baikal teal is migratory, wintering over on the flooded rice paddies of China and Japan.
Captivity: This is a lovely, small ornamental duck that is easy to keep, gregarious, and winter hardy. Birds reared in captivity in Europe are quite tame and calm. If several drakes live together, they engage in communal courtship displays in the spring.
Breeding: Offspring cannot regularly be expected, but breeding efforts on garden ponds have sometimes been successful. The nest is built in the cover of grass or other leafy plants, always close to the water but on dry ground. They will also use a concealed ground-level nest box. The breeding season is from the end of April to early July. A clutch of 6 to 9 grayish green eggs is incubated for 23 to 26 days. Rearing the baby ducklings is unproblematic. They are able to fly after 46 days and reach sexual maturity toward the end of their first year.

Blue-winged Teal

Anas discors

Size: 14½ to 16 inches (37–41 cm)
Origin: Across the middle of North America.
Description: The head of the drake is bluish gray with a black crown, forehead, and chin, and a bold white crescent starting above the eye and running down to the chin. The inner wing is powder blue, the speculum, green. The underparts are dark yellow densely covered with round, black spots, and there is a white patch on the rear flank. The bill is black and the legs, yellow. The female is brown with pale blue inner wings and a white abdomen.
Habitat: Shallow lakes that offer plenty of food; ponds with good landing sites; marshlands. Migratory birds.
Captivity: This is an attractively-colored small duck that is gregarious and easy to keep. It is ideal both for an aviary and for a garden pond, but it is not quite-winter hardy and needs a shelter for the cold season.
Breeding: Breeding this species presents no great problems. The nest is built close to the water but on dry ground and well hidden in dense vegetation. The breeding season is from late May to early June. A clutch of 7 to 10 white eggs is incubated 24 to 26 days. The baby ducklings are at first very shy. They are also sensitive to cold and dampness. The young birds are able to fly at about six weeks and reach breeding age at about ten months. If blue-winged and cinnamon teal are kept together, they often form mixed pairs.

Silver Teal

Anas versicolor

Size: 17 to 19 inches (43–48 cm)
Origin: In South America from Bolivia to the southern tip of Argentina; Falkland Islands.
Description: The two sexes are very similar. The crown is dark brown down to the eyes, as is the back of the neck and the nape. The rest of the head is cream-colored. The breast and abdomen are a muddy yellow densely dotted with dark brown. This pattern gradually changes to fine, dark brown barring on the sides of the abdomen and on the flanks. The upper parts are dark brown with a brown scallop pattern on the upper back. The speculum is an iridescent blue green bordered on both sides by white. The lower back down to the tail coverts shows a delicate black-and-white barring. The bill is pale blue with a black ridge and an orange-yellow spot at the base. The legs are gray. The female is slightly smaller, and the color contrasts on the head are less strong.

Drakes belonging to different ornamental species.
Above, left: Wood duck; above, right: Common or green-winged teal; center, left: European wigeon; center, right: Garganey; below, left: Northern shoveler; below, right: Pintail.

Habitat: Shallow lakes with plentiful food supply, especially in the pampas regions of Argentina.
Captivity: This is a handsomely colored small duck that is well suited for a garden pond or an aviary with a pond. It is gregarious, modest in its demands, and almost winter-hardy. Its nutritional needs are the same as those of other small ducks.
Breeding: Breeding this duck is not difficult. The breeding season starts in mid-April. The nest is built on dry ground in tall grass or other leafy plants. A clutch of 7 to 10 mud-yellow eggs is incubated for 24 to 26 days. It is best to rear the baby ducklings in a brooder. The young ducks are sexually mature by the end of their first year but usually don't breed until the second year.

Ringed Teal

Callonetta leucophrys

Size: 13¾ inches (35 cm)
Origin: From southern Brazil and southeastern Bolivia to Argentina.
Description: The drake has a black crown and nape; the rest of the head is off-white with delicate black shading. The mantle is grayish brown; the scapulars are bright chestnut-red; and the back, rump, and tail are black with a metallic green sheen. The wings are black with a large white patch on the wing coverts and a bronzish green speculum. The breast is pink with round, black dots. The flanks and abdomen are gray with delicate black barring, and the undertail coverts are black with a white spot on the side. The bill is bluish gray; the legs, pink. The female has a dark brown crown and a band of the same color below the eyes. The sides of the head are white with a light brown spot on the cheek. The shoulders are a muddy brown instead of the chestnut-red found on the male. The underparts are a dirty white with broad, brown cross-barring.
Habitat: Puddles and swamps in the light tropical forests that form the transition between rain forest and pampas.
Captivity: The ringed teal is an attractively colored small ornamental duck that is lively and gregarious. It is not winter-hardy and has to be kept at temperatures above freezing to keep it from losing its toes to frostbite. This duck should be kept only in aviaries and without curtailing its flying capacities. It likes to feed on soaked dried shrimp and small grains (millet, canary); in addition it should get high-protein pellets.
Breeding: This species nests in tree holes and needs nest boxes that are mounted well above ground. The breeding season starts at the end of May. A clutch of 4 to 8 white eggs is incubated for 23 days. Letting the natural mother rear the young has shown the best results. The baby ducklings need lots of warmth. Both parents share equally in the rearing of their offspring.

A pair of pintails shortly after mating.
The drake has just slipped off the female and is still holding on to the feathers on her head with his bill.

Bahama Pintail, White-cheeked Pintail, or Summer Duck

Anas bahamensis

Size: 13¾ to 15 inches (35–38 cm)
Origin: Caribbean Islands, South America, Galapagos Islands.
Description: Both sexes look alike. The cheeks, throat, and front of the neck are white; the rest of the plumage is yellowish brown with black markings. The speculum is an iridescent green, The tail is pointed and light-cinnamon colored. The bill is blue with a red patch at the base, and the legs are lead-gray.
Habitat: Puddles with plenty of vegetation, mangrove swamps, lagoons along the coast. Resident birds.
Captivity: This attractively colored, small tropical duck is gregarious and modest in its demands but not winter-hardy. It is well suited for an aviary or a small garden pond.

The Bahama pintail is a small tropical duck that does well if kept in aviaries or small garden ponds.

Breeding: This species is easy to breed and likes nest boxes best. In Europe its breeding season is in April or May. A clutch consists of 8 to 12 mud-colored eggs that are incubated for 25 to 26 days. The female is a reliable brooder and rears the ducklings by herself. The young are ready to fly at six to seven weeks and reach sexual maturity by the end of the year but don't start breeding until the second year.

Mandarin Duck

Aix galericulata

Size: 17 inches (43 cm)
Origin: The Far East; introduced into southern England.
Description: The drake is very striking with dramatic color contrasts on the head, a crest of long feathers on the nape, small orange "wing sails" on the back, a red bill, and yellow legs. The female is inconspicuous, having grayish brown upper parts, marbled light underparts, and a white line running from the eye to the nape. Her bill is gray.
Habitat: Ponds, lakes, and slow-moving rivers in deciduous forests, none of them with abundant food sources; also, mountain lakes in evergreen forests. Migratory birds.
Captivity: The mandarin duck is one of the most spectacular small ornamental ducks and is reminiscent of Chinese and Japanese painting. Since it is winter-hardy in central Europe and has modest nutritional demands, it is an ideal duck for garden ponds there as well as for aviaries. If kept on waters in well-wooded parks, mandarin ducks don't need to have their flying powers restrained. If you want to keep the ducks from migrating in the winter, they have to have open water and sufficient food. If mandarin ducks are kept together with other ducks, the drakes unfortunately have a tendency to be aggressive and pursue and rape females. During the breeding season in the spring, the drakes perform impressive communal courtship displays. This species likes to feed on tender plant material and can jump 3 feet straight up in the air in order to reach tempting greenery.

Breeding: Breeding mandarin ducks is easy. They are pure hole nesters that never build nests in the open and always require nest boxes. In their native habitat they use tree holes made by woodpeckers and hollow tree sections that are often 30 to 60 feet (10–20 m) off the ground. If you keep these ducks on a garden pond or in an aviary, the nest boxes should be 20 inches (50 cm) above the ground, and a small ladder should lead up to the entry hole so that birds with clipped wings can get to the nest. Since female mandarin ducks do not pluck feathers from their breasts to line the nest, the bottom of the nest cavity should be covered with sawdust, peat moss, or dry leaves. The breeding season is from late April to early May. A clutch of 8 to 12 creamy white eggs is incubated for 31 days. The newly hatched ducklings climb up the vertical walls of the nest cavity, using their needle-sharp claws, and then drop to the ground, where the mother is waiting for them and leads them to the water in a group. Since the baby ducklings weigh less than an ounce (25 g) and their bones are still soft and elastic, they land on the forest floor from heights up to 50 or 60 feet without harm. The ducklings are able to fly after 63 days. The young males acquire their nuptial plumage in the fall of their first year, and the females lay eggs after one year. Usually, however, the eggs are not fertile until the end of the second year. Female mandarin ducks and female wood ducks look rather similar, and if both species are kept together, crossbreeding is common. The offspring, however, are always infertile.

Wood Duck or Carolina Duck

Aix sponsa

Size: 17 to 20 inches (43–51 cm)
Origin: Eastern North Amerca, Cuba.
Description: The drake is brightly colored above, with a long, curving crest, a bold white chin spot, and a red bill. The legs are yellow. The female has a gray crest and a wide, white eye ring that extends in a pointed line behind the eye. Otherwise she closely resembles the female mandarin duck (see page 00).
Habitat: Small ponds and rivers in wooded country. Visits freshwater marshes in the late summer and fall. In northern breeding areas wood ducks are migratory.
Captivity: This duck is hardly less spectacular than the mandarin duck. Like the latter, it is winter-hardy in central Europe and has modest demands. And it is less aggressive. Wood ducks do not engage in communal courtship displays, but the courtship ritual with which the drake woos his mate is quite striking. He sometimes even offers her tidbits of food, a courtship display that is extremely rare in ducks. Wood ducks are quite friendly toward their caretakers, but if they are not fenced, they can do considerable damage to young plants in a garden. Wood ducks are not as well suited to flying freely in large parks as mandarin ducks, because they often migrate to warmer climates in the fall and fail to return in the spring. Crossbreeding with many other species of ornamental ducks is common. Unfortunately the coloring of hybrid offspring is always much duller than that of normal wood duck drakes.
Breeding: Breeding wood ducks in captivity is often successful. The breeding season starts in April. Wood ducks are hole nesters that brood in tree holes, and their needs are the same as those of mandarin ducks (see page 82). A clutch consists of 15 creamy white eggs, which are incubated for 28 to 32 days. If the eggs are removed, a duck may lay up to 30 eggs in a breeding season. These eggs can be given to a call duck (see page 91) for brooding, or they can be artificially incubated. The baby ducklings can easily climb up on vertical wire mesh with their sharp claws, and their rearing cages therefore have to be enclosed with wire mesh at the top, too. The ducklings are independent at six weeks and able to fly at nine weeks.

By the time they are four-and-a-half months old young wood ducks resemble adult birds. The females already lay fertile eggs when they are one year old.

Ornamental Ducks: Diving Ducks

Diving ducks swim with their bodies lower in the water than dabbling ducks, and their legs are set farther back on the body, close to the tail end. They dive with a quick jerk and feed at the bottom, often many feet below the water's surface.

Red-crested Pochard

Netta rufina

Size: 21¾ inches (55 cm)
Origin: From central Eurasia eastward to western Siberia.
Description: The drake has a bushy, erectile, golden-orange crest, and the rest of the head and the upper neck are fox-red. The lower neck and the breast are black. The flanks, a band on the shoulder, and the underside of the wings are white. The bill, eyes, and feet are red. The female is brown with conspicuously light cheeks.
Habitat: Large, warm, shallow lakes and ponds

with lush vegetation. Migratory birds.
Captivity: This is the largest diving duck found in Europe. It is very decorative, modest in its demands, and winter-hardy. In the spring five or six drakes often perform a communal courtship display. Later the drake may engage in courtship-feeding of his mate. The drakes are aggressive only in the spring; later they are peaceable. Red-crested pochards are vegeterians and have many traits in common with dabbling ducks, such as cropping the grass in a meadow. If they are kept on a small garden pond, they should, if possible, not be combined with other species. Red-crested pochards can live up to 15 years in captivity.

Breeding: Breeding this species is easy. The ducks accept nest houses and nest boxes, and the drake keeps guard near the nest. The eggs are laid in early May. They are grayish yellow, and there are between 6 and 12 in a clutch, which is incubated 26 to 28 days. The ducklings are aggressive and rough with ducklings of other species. Rearing them presents no problems, especially if there is some duckweed to supplement their diet. They are able to fly at 26 to 27 days and reach sexual maturity toward the end of the year.

Rosy-bill

Netta peposaca

Size: 22¾ inches (58 cm)
Origin: Southern South America.
Description: The drake keeps his nuptial plumage all year. His head, neck, and breast are black with a purple sheen to it; the upper parts are black, and the underparts, gray. The bill and a nublike enlargement at its base are a bright pink to red. The eyes are orange-red, and the legs are yellowish. The female can be distinguished from a female red-crested pochard by her overall dark brown coloring and her whitish chin.
Habitat: Small, shallow lakes with plenty of vegetation in the pampas; lakes with reedy shores near the coast. Migratory birds.
Captivity: This is a decorative species that is peaceable, modest in its demands, and winter-hardy. A single pair can be kept on a small garden pond, but larger ponds are a better environment for them. Rosy-bills, which are largely vegetarian, graze on meadows and like tender young plant parts. It is therefore not advisable to let them run loose near your flower beds. Rosy-bills tend to interbreed with red-crested pochards and other diving ducks.
Breeding: Breeding rosy-bills is easy. They nest on dry ground among grass and other leafy plants, but they also accept nest boxes and nest houses. Egg-laying starts in mid-May. A clutch consists of 10 to 12 grayish green eggs, which are incubated 27 to 29 days. The females are reliable brooders and excellent mothers. The baby ducklings are robust and easy to rear. The young drakes get their adult plumage toward the end of their first year, but the females don't start laying until they are almost 2 years old.

European Pochard

Aythya ferina

Size: 17¾ inches (45 cm)
Origin: Northern Eurasia from Great Britain eastward to Mongolia.
Description: The head and neck of the European pochard are chestnut red; the back and flanks, light gray; and the breast and tail feathers, black. The bill is grayish blue with black at the base and tip. The eyes are red; the legs, dark gray. The female is grayish brown with a darker brown on the head, neck, and breast.
Habitat: Reedy inland waters with plenty of food. Migratory birds.
Captivity: This decorative duck, which is gregarious, modest in its demands, and winter-hardy, should be kept only on larger bodies of water, not on small garden ponds or on swimming basins in aviaries. It needs water at least 28 inches (70 cm) deep for diving. European pochards can live as long as 20 to 22 years in captivity.
Breeding: Breeding pochards is possible only on

large park ponds. The breeding season is in May and June. Nests are built amid leafy vegetation or reeds, but nest houses and nest boxes are accepted, too. A clutch consists of 8 to 11 grayish green eggs and is incubated for 24 to 26 days. The females are reliable brooders and good mothers. Rearing these ducklings presents no problems, especially if duckweed is available. The ducklings are able to fly at 55 days and reach sexual maturity toward the end of their first year.

Tufted Duck

Aythya fuligula

Size: 17 inches (43 cm)
Origin: Northern Eurasia and eastward to the Pacific Ocean.
Description: The drake is primarily black above with a pointed crest on the back of the head, which has a purple tinge. The eyes are light yellow; the flanks and abdomen, white. The bill is bluish gray, and the legs are lead gray. The female is an almost uniform blackish brown with only a hint of a crest.
Habitat: Large, still, or slowly moving waters with small islands and lush vegetation along the shores. On waters that stay open during the winter, tufted ducks are resident.
Captivity: This species is decorative, lively, peaceable, modest in its demands, and winter-hardy, but it can be kept only on larger ponds and needs at least 28 inches (70 cm) of water for diving. It feeds primarily on molluscs, which it dives up to 40 feet (12 m) to find. Tufted ducks can live up to 18 years and longer in captivity.
Breeding: Attempts to breed tufted ducks are not always successful. The breeding season is from mid-May to mid-June. This duck accepts nest boxes only reluctantly and prefers to build her nests hidden in dense vegetation close to the water. A clutch consists of 8 to 10 grayish green eggs, which are incubated 23 to 25 days. The baby ducklings are independent after just a few days and pay little attention to their mother from that point on. They are able to fly at eight to nine weeks and grow their

The tufted duck can be kept only on larger ponds, needing water at least 28 inches (70 cm) deep for diving.

adult plumage during the first fall, but successful breeding is not likely until the second year.

Ferruginous Duck

Aythya nyroca

Size: 15¾ inches (40 cm)
Origin: From southern Europe and northern Africa eastward to western Siberia and Mongolia. Rarely breeds in central Europe.
Description: The drake is mahogany brown with white under tail coverts and white eyes. The female is dark brown with a red sheen; she has dark eyes.
Habitat: Shallow ponds with lush vegetation offering plenty of food. Migratory birds.
Captivity: This is the smallest European diving duck. It is easy to keep, modest in its demands, winter-hardy, has a lively nature, and becomes tame quickly. Pairs are sometimes aggressive toward other diving ducks during the reproductive cycle. Garden ponds have to be at least 32 inches (80 cm) deep but are still not ideal for ferruginous ducks. These ducks thrive better on park ponds with lush vegetation.
Breeding: Breeding this species is quite possible. The breeding season is from mid-May to mid-June.

Ferruginous ducks prefer to build their nests hidden in dense vegetation along the edge of the water, but they will also accept nest houses and nest boxes. A clutch consists of 7 to 11 light gray to yellow eggs, which are incubated 25 to 27 days. The baby ducklings are robust and easy to rear. They are able to fly at 56 to 60 days and reach sexual maturity toward the end of their first year.

Ruddy Duck or North American Ruddy Duck

Oxyura jamaicensis

Size: 14½ to 16 inches (37–41 cm)
Origin: Western and central North America; Central America; from northwestern South America south as far as Tierra del Fuego.
Description: The drake has a black head and neck, white cheeks, and a pale blue bill. The breast, back, and flanks are chestnut red; the abdomen, a muddy brown mixed with white; the undertail coverts, white; the pointed tail, grayish brown; and the legs, dark blue. The female is brownish gray with a dark brown crown and a stripe of the same color crossing the light cheek from the base of the lower mandible to the ear region. The bill and the legs are a dark grayish blue.

Habitat: Shallow waters with lush vegetation offering plenty of food. Migratory in the northern area of distribution.

Captivity: This is a charming small diving duck, gregarious, lively, winter-hardy, and modest in its food demands. Ruddy ducks have been bred in captivity with some frequency in recent years and are often available for sale. Since this species does not like to leave the water, the food dishes should be placed at the edge of the water. Or you can offer grains like millet, wheat, and barley in dishes on the water. Duckweed is very popular with ruddy ducks.

Breeding: Breeding ruddy ducks is not difficult. Offer nest sites in the form of a hollow in the ground that is filled with dry leaves or a flat fruit crate placed among vegetation right next to the water. The breeding season is in mid-May. A clutch consists of 6 to 12 very large, whitish eggs with thick shells. Incubation lasts 23 to 26 days. The big, strong baby ducklings are first led by both parents, later just by the mother. They are able to fly at 52 to 60 days and are ready to breed at 10 to 12 months.

Common Goldeneye or European Goldeneye

Bucephala clangula

Size: 18 inches (46 cm)
Origin: Northern Eurasia and North America.
Description: The drake has a large, almost triangular-looking, greenish black head with a large white spot beside the black bill and below the light yellow eye. The upper parts are black except for the scapulars, which are white with diagonal black lines. The underparts are white, and the legs are yellow. The female is smaller than the male and has a brown head, a white neck ring, and a grayish brown body.
Habitat: Large ponds with clear water. Migratory birds.
Captivity: This attractive and lively diving duck sometimes teases other kinds of ducks but never harms them. The drake engages in complex courtship displays, during which the head is tossed back

The common goldeneye is one of the tree breeding ducks. It is an attractive and lively diving duck.

onto the rump. These ducks need food that is high in animal proteins, such as shrimp, pieces of fish, and ground meat. In addition, they should be fed wheat grain, pellets for turkeys, and finely chopped greens. Common goldeneyes can live 15 to 20 years in captivity. They are winter-hardy.
Breeding: Goldeneyes can be bred only on largish ponds or on garden ponds with clear, clean water. A breeding pair should be kept by itself. The breeding season is from mid-March to early May. A clutch consists of 8 to 10 bluish green eggs, which are incubated 27 to 32 days. Goldeneyes brood their eggs only in nest boxes that are suspended above ground. The baby ducklings leave the nest hole by letting themselves drop to the ground. If they are reared artificially, they easily climb up the walls of boxes or of wire mesh by using their sharp claws. Rearing them is not altogether simple. They need a rearing ration high in proteins. A starter diet made up of starter ration for duck or turkey chicks, cooked and ground beef heart, dry cottage cheese, duckweed, mosquito larvae, and mealworms is recommended. The ducklings are able to fly at eight weeks and reach sexual maturity at two years. Successful breeding results cannot be expected until the third year.

Utility Ducks: Heavyweight Breeds

American Pekin Duck

Origin: This breed was developed in the United States around 1870 by crossing Aylesbury ducks with stock of Chinese origin. In Europe, American Pekin ducks have been bred since the beginning of this century.
Description: Weight of drake: 7¾pounds (3.5 kg); female: 6½ pounds (3 kg). This duck has a deep body that looks almost like a square with rounded edges. The body is carried with the front slightly raised on legs of medium height. The plumage is pure white.
Eggs: White to yellowish. Minimum weight: 2.5 ounces (70 g). Annual production: 100 to 130 eggs.
Special Remarks: This is the most common commerical duck raised in Germany for both meat and eggs. Its ratio of converting feed into meat is very high, and no other breed grows faster. Eight-week-old ducklings weigh 2¼ to 5½ pounds (1–2.5 kg) if fed properly. American Pekin ducks can be kept relatively closely confined and without water for swimming.

The German Pekin duck is a utility duck bred for both meat and eggs.

German Pekin Duck

Origin: The original stock was imported to England and Germany from the Far East, and the present strain was developed in Germany.
Description: Weight of drake: 7¾ pounds (3.5 kg); female: 6½ pounds (3 kg). This duck has an upright posture and a blocky, square body with an upswept tail. The legs are short and sturdy, and the plumage is white with a yellowish tinge.
Eggs: White to yellowish. Minimum weight: 2.5 ounces (70 g). Annual production: 100 to 130 eggs.
Special Remarks: This is a good meat duck. The young birds grow quickly and are hardy. This duck can therefore be bred even in a harsh climate. It thrives best outdoors with plentiful access to water.

The German Pekin is the best meat producer of all the white ducks and also yields lots of feathers.

Aylesbury Duck

Origin: This breed was developed in England as a market duck.
Description: Weight of drake: 7¾ pounds (3.5 kg); female: 6½ pounds (3 kg). This is a deep-bodied but not plump-looking duck with horizontal carriage. The plumage is white.
Eggs: White to greenish. Minimum weight: 2.8 ounces (80 g). Annual production: up to 100 eggs.
Special Remarks: In terms of size and heaviness, this is probably the best commercial duck. Its meat is tender, white, and exceptionally tasty. For best development this duck needs to be able to run free and should have a place to swim.

Rouen Duck

Origin: This duck was originally developed in the Rouen area of France from local farm ducks. The breed's present size and coloring are the result of selective breeding in England. The Rouen duck was introduced into Germany around 1850.
Description: Weight of drake: 7¾ pounds (3.5 kg); female: 6½ pounds (3 kg). The Rouen duck is a beautifully colored and nobly shaped large duck with a calm nature. It embodies the square shape that breeders of meat ducks aim for. The recognized color strains are "wild," which is equivalent to the natural coloring of the mallard duck (see page 72), and "blue wild," in which the parts that are black in the "wild" strain are blue.
Eggs: Green, sometimes lighter (whitish) or darker (bluish). Minimum weight: 2.8 ounces (80 g). Annual production: 60 to 90 eggs.
Special Remarks: Rouen ducks have a calm temperament and become quite tame. They can be kept successfully in a relatively small space without swimming opportunity. When raised for market, they can reach a weight of 11 pounds (5 kg). The meat is somewhat darker than that of the previously described breeds, but it has an excellent flavor and is tender and juicy. The Rouen is not a good laying duck, and raising Rouen ducklings requires a little more effort during the first few weeks than raising other breeds. The baby ducklings have to be protected especially against getting wet from above (rain).

Saxony Duck

Origin: This strain was originally developed in Germany in the 1930s and revived in the 1950s by crossing Rouen, German Pekin, and Pommern ducks.
Description: Weight of drake: 7¾ pounds (3.5 kg); female: 6½ pounds (3 kg). This is a sturdy utility duck with a long, broad body without any keel formation and with an almost horizontal carriage. The drake has a pigeon-blue head and neck and an unbroken white neck ring. The breast, lower neck, and shoulders are rusty red. The breast feathers are lightly edged with silver, the rump is pigeon-blue, and the wings are flour-colored. The female has a dark yellow head, neck, and breast. The wing coverts are cream-colored with a slight bluish tinge and a pigeon-blue speculum. There is also a light stripe above the eyes and a hint of a neck ring.
Eggs: White. Minimum weight: 2.8 ounces (80 g). Annual production: 100 to 140 eggs.
Special Remarks: The Saxony has all the traits of an ideal duck. Its unusual coloring is a challenge to any breeder, and the duck's economic return is significant. The young birds grow fast, and if they are fed for market, they are generally ready for slaughter at 10 weeks. Their egg production is also quite impressive.

Utility Ducks: Medium-weight Breeds

Cayuga Duck

Origin: This breed originated in the United States and is named after Lake Cayuga in New York State.

It was introduced to Germany via England around 1870.

Description: Weight of drake: 6½ pounds (3 kg); female: 5½ pounds (2.5 kg). This is a medium-sized duck with an almost horizontal carriage and a nicely rounded shape. Both sexes are black with a green metallic luster on the head, neck, and back, and with a bright blue speculum.

Eggs: Pure white to dark green. Minimum weight: 2.3 ounces (65 g). Annual production: 70 to 100 eggs.

Special remarks: The Cayuga is a calm, friendly, and hardy duck, but it is not suitable for confined quarters. The taste of the meat is similar to that of mallards. The carcass is meaty, and the skin is pure white. Raising ducklings is unproblematic.

Gimbsheim Duck

Origin: This breed was developed between 1958 and 1963 in Gimbsheim in southwestern West Germany. It is the result of crossing Orpington, American Pekin, and Saxony ducks.

Description: Weight of drake: 6½ pounds (3 kg); female: 5½ pounds (2.5 kg). This breed is large for a medium-weight duck, with a long, broad body that does not look plump. The carriage is almost horizontal, with a slight backward tilt. Both sexes are a rich bluish green with a darker head and neck.

Eggs: Yellowish to green. Minimum weight: 2.5 ounces (70 g). Annual production: about 100 eggs.

Special remarks: This duck has a good market potential and has interesting coloring. Its meat is excellent. It is not suitable for confined quarters.

Altrhein Magpie Duck

Origin: This breed is of recent origin (around 1970) and was also developed in Gimbsheim, southwestern West Germany.

Description: Weight of drake: 6½ pounds (3 kg); female: 5½ pounds (2.5 kg). The body is sturdy; the carriage, somewhat raised; and the legs, medium long. The plumage of both sexes is pure white with regular black markings on the crown, the back, the shoulders, and the upper tail coverts.

Eggs: White to light green. Minimum weight: 2.3 ounces (65 g). Annual production: around 100 eggs.

Special Remarks: This new breed has interesting coloring as well as good meat quality and a capacity for gaining weight for market. It is not suitable for confined quarters.

Altrhein Magpie Duck

Origin: This breed is of recent origin (around 1970) and was also developed in Gimbsheim, southwestern West Germay.

Description: Weight of drake: 6½ pounds (3 kg); female: 5½ pounds (2.5 kg). the body is sturdy; the carriage, somewhat raised; and the legs, medium long. The plumage of both sexes is pure white with regular black markings on the crown, the back, the shoulder, and the upper tail coverts.

Eggs: White to light green. Minimum weight: 2.3 ounces (65 g). Annual production: around 100 eggs.

Special Remarks: This new breed has interesting coloring as well as good meat quality and a capacity for gaining weight for market. It is not suitable for confined quarters.

Orpington Duck

Origin: This breed originated in England around 1880.

Description: Weight of drake: 6½ pounds (3 kg); female: 5½ pounds (2.5 kg). This is a lively, medium-heavy duck with a cylindrical body and moderately upright carriage. The drake has a chocolate-brown head and neck; the rest of the plumage is a uniform yellowish brown. The female is yellowish brown all over.

Eggs: Pure white to green. Minimum weight: 2.3 ounces (65 g). Annual production: 150 to 180 eggs.

Special Remarks: This is one of the best utility ducks, and it can be kept in relatively crowded quarters. Orpingtons do not need a place to swim, but they do have to be able to bathe. This breed is probably the most modest in its food needs. The meat is very tender and juicy. The Orpington is also a good laying duck, starting to lay in December and continuing until August. The taste of the eggs is excellent and very similar to that of chicken eggs. Ducklings are easy to raise.

Pommern Duck

Origin: This breed was developed from local farm ducks in Pomerania in northeastern Europe, the area where most Pommern ducks used to be raised.
Description: Weight of drake: 3½ pounds (3 kg); female: 5½ pounds (2.5 kg). This breed has a long, broad, and deep body that does not appear plump in spite of its size and is carried horizontally. Two color strains are recognized: blue and black. The plumage is the same for both sexes. The blue strain is an even light blue with a white bib on the upper breast. There is no speculum. The black strain is slate black with a pronounced green luster. This strain, too, has a white bib.
Eggs: Bluish green. Medium weight: 2.5 ounces (70 g). Annual production: 90 to 120 eggs.
Special Remarks: This is an excellent utility duck with good meat production. The ducklings are hardy, fast growing, and reach market weight at 10 weeks. The meat is very tasty. The requirements of this breed are modest, but the ducks thrive best in a large run with a place for swimming.

Utility Ducks: Lightweight Breeds

Campbell Duck

Origin: This strain was developed in England for egg production.
Description: Weight of drake: 5½ pounds (2.5 kg); female: 4½ pounds (2 kg). This lightly built but not slim duck has a somewhat upright carriage. There are two color strains: khaki and white. The plumage is the same in both sexes. The khaki strain has a dark brown head and neck with a green luster; the rest of the plumage is khaki with a reddish tinge. The speculum is brown. The white strain of this lightweight utility breed is pure white all over.
Eggs: White to greenish. Minimum weight: 2.3 ounces (65 g). Annual production: 180 to 200 eggs.
Special Remarks: The Campbell duck is easy to raise, matures early, is hardy, and is an enormously productive layer. These qualities make it one of the best utility ducks. Production is highest if the birds have a generous run, but water for swimming is not absolutely necessary.

Indian Runner Duck

Origin: This duck goes back to stock from eastern and southeastern Asia with the same upright "penguin" posture. The first Indian runners were brought to England in the nineteenth century, and many varieties have been developed in Germany in this century.
Description: Weight of drake: 4½ pounds (2 kg); female: 4 pounds (1.75 kg). The Indian runner is a symmetrically built, trim, very slender duck with very upright carriage. Eight color varieties are recognized in the Federal Republic of Germany: wild color, trout, white, black, brown, blue, fawn and white, and pea yellow.
Eggs: Mostly white; somewhat greenish in darker strains of birds. Minimum weight: 2.3 ounces (65 g). Annual production: 200 eggs.
Special Remarks: This "greyhound" among ducks is very lively and agile as well as hardy. It is not a meat duck but excels at egg-laying. Indian runners can be bred in a confined area, but the results are much better if the ducks have a largish run. They don't need to swim but do have to have a place to bathe. This duck is especially recommended for breeders of utility ducks in a relatively urban environment.

Crested Duck

Origin: The crested duck is a mutation of European farm ducks that has been around for centuries.
Description: Weight of drake: 5½ pounds (2.5 kg); female: 4½ pounds (2 kg). The crested duck is a

sturdy farm duck (a farm duck is a utility duck of no particular breed) with a ball-shaped crest on the back of the head, a noticeably bent neck, and a horizontal carriage. All colors and markings are recognized. The crest should be of good size and not lopsided or divided.
Eggs: White; rarely greenish. Minimum weight: 2.1 ounces (60 g). Annual production: approximately 120 eggs.
Special Remarks: This lively, friendly, and hardy duck is the prototype of Walt Disney's Donald Duck. It needs a place to swim. The ducklings are easy to raise and mature early. The quality of the meat is good, and the laying season lasts from January to July.

High-nesting Flying Duck

Origin: German breeders developed this strain early in this century by crossing domestic ducks with wild mallards. The ability to fly and the habit of nesting high above ground were retained.
Description: Weight of drake: 3⅓ pounds (1.5 kg); female: 2¾ pounds (1.25 kg). This duck is slightly larger and more compact than a wild mallard. All colors recognized in standards for heavyweight ducks are accepted, as well as light and dark wild coloring and crested individuals.
Eggs: Greenish. Minimum weight: 1.75 ounces (50 g). Annual production: 30 to 36 eggs in two separate clutches.
Special remarks: This lively, hardy strain that enjoys flying can be kept unrestrained on water near a farm. The ducks like to nest in tree holes up to 11 feet (3.5 m) above ground, but they will also brood on the ground. To prevent the ducks from going wild, you should get them accustomed to their shelters by feeding them there every evening. Since this strain lives largely on what it can forage for itself, it is cheaper to maintain than other breeds. Don't keep these ducks near fish hatcheries! Undesired crossings with wild mallards are unfortunately common. The females incubate and lead their offspring reliably. They also make good foster mothers for ornamental ducklings. The ducklings grow fast, reaching a weight of 3 ⅓ pounds (1.5 kg) in 8 to 10 weeks. October is the best time to butcher them because the ducks are well nourished then. The meat is tender and tasty, and there is a good market for it.

East Indie Duck

Origin: United States. No details known. The East Indie was introduced to England around 1850 and was brought to Germany from there.
Description: Weight of drake: 2¼ pounds (1 kg); female: 1½ pounds (.75 kg). The East Indie is a small duck with a plump, round body and a slightly raised carriage. The plumage of both sexes is coal black with an iridescent-green sheen.
Eggs: Dark green, becoming lighter as the laying season progresses. Minimum weight: 1.9 ounces (55 g). Annual production: up to 80 eggs.
Special Remarks: This is an elegant, lively miniature duck of no economic significance. East Indies are kept primarily for esthetic enjoyment. The females incubate and lead their offspring reliably and can therefore be used as foster mothers for ornamental breeds.

Call Duck

Origin: This breed was originally developed in England to serve as a decoy in duck hunting.
Description: Weights much over 2 pounds (1 kg) are undesirable. This is a miniature breed with a short body, a round head with full cheeks, a short bill, and a low, horizontal carriage. All the colors recognized in large breeds are accepted both with and without a crest.
Eggs: White to greenish. Minimum weight: 1.4 ounces (40 g). Annual production: about 60 eggs.
Special Remarks: This is a very lively and undemanding domestic duck of no economic importance. It can be used to incubate and rear the baby ducklings of ornamental species. It is frequently kept on park waters, where crosses of wild Mallards and Call Ducks are also commonly seen.

Ornamental Ducks and Utility Ducks

Muscovy Duck

Origin: This strain was originally domesticated from the wild muscovy duck (*Cairina moschata*) by the Indians in the rain forests of South America. It was brought to Europe by the Spaniards.

Description: Weight of drake: 8¾ pounds (4 kg); female: 6½ pounds (3 kg). This is a large duck with big, red caruncles on the face. The long, very broad body is carried horizontally. It is broad but not very deep, and there is no keel formation. The tail is long. In the wild form, both sexes are black with a green and blue luster and white wing coverts. In the Federal Republic of Germany, six color strains of the domestic muscovy are recognized: wild coloring, blue and wild, pearl gray, black, white, and magpie.

Eggs: White, often with a yellow tinge. Minimum weight: 2.5 ounces (70 g). Annual production: 80 to 100 eggs.

Special Remarks: Muscovies are fed and maintained like other domestic ducks. They like to graze and are somewhat sensitive to the cold. They are good fliers and brood two or three times a year in nest boxes hung high. Nest boxes set up inside shelters should be raised, too. Indoors, muscovies start laying as early as January or February; outdoors, somewhat later. The ducks brood and rear their young reliably, and therefore they also make good foster mothers for ornamental ducklings. The drakes are often aggressive, chase other poultry, and rape other domestic female ducks. Muscovy ducks are excellent meat producers with a high proportion of breast meat. They can also be fattened for market. Young drakes should be butchered at 11 to 12 weeks; young females are best at 10 weeks. The meat is darkish but of excellent taste. Muscovies can be crossed with other domestic ducks. The offspring are not fertile but have good meat.

Useful Addresses and Literature

Principal Authorities responsible for CITES Licensing (see page 47)

United States of America
Chief of the Federal Wildlife Permit Office,
Room 611, Broyhill Building,
1000 North Glebe Road,
Arlington, VA 22201
Telephone (703) 235-2418

Australia
Australian National Parks and Wildlife Services,
PO Box 636
Canberra A.C.T. 2601
Telephone (062) 466211

Canada
The Administrator,
Convention on International Trade in Endangered Species
Canadian Wildlife Service,
Department of the Environment,
Ottawa, Ontario K1A 0E7
Telephone (819) 997-1840

South Africa
Department of Environmental Affairs
Environmental Conservation Division
Private Bag X 447,
Pretoria 0001
Telephone 299-2567

United Kingdom
Department of the Environment,
Tollgate House,
Houlton Street,
Bristol BS2 9DJ
Telephone 0272-218811

Books

Handbook of Waterfowl Behaviour, Paul A. Johnsgard. Constable, London, 1965.

Life Histories of North American Waterfowl, Arthur Cleveland Bent. Dover, New York, 1962.

The New Wildfowler in the 1970s, edited by Noel M. Sedgewick, Peter Whitaker and Jeffery Harrison. Barrie and Jenkins, London, 1970.

Ornamental Waterfowl, A. A. Johnson and W. H. Payn. Witherby, London, 1968.

Travels and Traditions of Waterfowl, H. Albert Hochbaum. University of Minnesota Press, Minneapolis, 1955.

The Waterfowl of the World, Jean Delacour. Country Life, London, 1954-1964.

Waterfowl Tomorrow, edited by Joseph P. Linduska. U.S. Department of the Interior, Washington, 1964.

Index

Numbers in *italics* indicate color plates; C1, front cover; C2, inside front cover; C3, inside back cover; C4, back cover.